PEACE SMIL
REDISCOVERING THOM.   ₋ᴋTON

PEACE SMILES

Rediscovering Thomas Merton

BISHOP FINTAN MONAHAN

VERITAS

Published 2020 by
Veritas Publications
7–8 Lower Abbey Street
Dublin 1
publications@veritas.ie
veritas.ie

ISBN 978 1 84730 970 9

A catalogue record for this book is available from the British Library.

Opening quote taken from a letter from Thomas Merton to
Pope John XXIII, 10 November 1958; quoted in Jim Forest,
Living with Wisdom: A Life of Thomas Merton,
New York: Orbis Books, 2008, p. 143.
All quotations of Thomas Merton's poetry taken from
The Collected Poems of Thomas Merton, New York: New Directions, 1977.
Used with kind permission.

Design and typesetting by Colette Dower, Veritas Publications
Cover image: Painting of Thomas Merton by Harry Guinnane,
after a photograph of Thomas Merton by John Lyons.
Used with kind permission.

Printed in the Republic of Ireland by SPRINT-print Ltd, Dublin

My dear Holy Father,
It seems to me that, as a contemplative,
I do not need to lock myself into solitude and lose all contact
with the rest of the world; rather this poor world has a right
to a place in my solitude.

Letter from Thomas Merton to Pope John XXIII,
10 November 1958

Contents

Foreword

In 2015, Pope Francis said of the Trappist monk and bestselling author:

> Merton was above all a man of prayer, a thinker, who challenged the certitudes of his time and opened new horizons for souls and for the Church. He was also a man of dialogue, a promoter of peace between peoples and religions.[1]

Bishop Fintan Monahan has gone a long way in *Peace Smiles* to explain why Thomas Merton remains so appealing and relevant and why his prophetic and socially engaged voice must be rediscovered and heard now more than ever. Bishop Monahan's beautiful, reader-friendly and straightforward introduction to Merton's life and writings provides a timely reminder that Thomas Merton remains a compelling prophet for our times. *Peace Smiles* traces Thomas Merton's fascinating and sometimes troubled life from a disrupted childhood and rather turbulent adolescence, to his conversion to Roman Catholicism whilst at university in the US and eventual ordination in 1949 at the Trappist Abbey of Gethsemani. It was then that Merton's prophetic voice began to emerge. Bishop Monahan also explores Merton as artist, social critic and ecumenist, as well as his anti-war and anti-racist stances until his untimely death at the age of fifty-three due to accidental electrocution.

Bishop Monahan shows us, above all, that a profound hope breathes within Merton's writing that we too can find our way home by remaining authentic and true to ourselves. Merton wrote, 'For me to be a saint means to be myself.

Therefore, the problem of sanctity and salvation is in fact the problem of finding out who I am and of discovering my true self.'[2] As Bishop Monahan shows, this quest for authenticity and truth became a lifelong search for Merton. Merton highlights constantly the importance of the individual and the personal inner journey that leads to authenticity and to the Universal.

I have been fascinated by Thomas Merton since I discovered, over twenty years ago, that frequently during his Asian journey, he wrote in the margins of his journal, 'Eckhart is my life raft, Eckhart is my life raft.'[3] In *Conjectures of a Guilty Bystander* Thomas Merton praises Meister Eckhart as one of the prodigious voices that 'sang [him] into the church'. In many of his writings, Thomas Merton emphasised the importance of interiority. Following Meister Eckhart, Merton advocates journeying deep within ourselves, to the authentic ground of our being which is the ground of our soul and where we become one with the Ground of God, the groundless ground and one with universal humanity. It is also the sense of the beautiful lines in scripture where God says through the prophet Hosea (2:14), that he will lead his beloved, the noble soul, out into the desert, and there he will speak to her in her heart, 'one with One, one from One, one in One and a single One eternally'.[4] This language permeated much of Merton's writings. In his first letter to Boris Pasternak, for example, Merton wrote, 'It is as if we met on a deeper level of life on which individuals are not separate beings.'[5] Jean Sulivan, a French priest, born two years before Thomas Merton, wrote an article in *Le Monde* in 1970 on the absolute importance of Merton's prodigious writings in helping us to find *un langage d'intériorité*, the language of interiority.[6] Sulivan travelled to India in 1964, where he had a mystical experience after an encounter with the French Benedictine monk, Henri Le Saux, whose vocation was to live out the Christian-Hindu encounter on a profound level. In India, Sulivan, like Merton, discovered the importance of spiritual detachment.

As Bishop Monahan has shown, Merton wrote arguably his most beautiful lines about the subject of solitude:

So much do I love this solitude that when I walk out among the roads to the old barns that stand alone, far from the new buildings, delight begins to overpower me from head to foot and peace smiles even in the marrow of my bones.[7]

Again following Meister Eckhart, Merton advocates here a wandering or errant joy, where one may remain outwardly active, but is in a state of perpetual awareness of one's divine calling and belonging. Reiner Schürmann calls this a 'wandering identity' between the creature and God.[8] The proof of attainment of the birth of God in the soul, according to Eckhart, is that the person is in a state of permanent awareness of the divine in all things and in all persons. For Thomas Merton, all things provided a 'glimpse of the cosmic dance'.[9]

Thomas Aquinas wrote in the *Summa Contra Gentiles*, 'Since God is the universal cause of all Being, in whatever region Being can be found, there must be the Divine Presence.'[10] Eckhart's whole claim ultimately depends on man's possession of pure being in the spark or apex of the soul. Merton wrote in *Conjectures of a Guilty Bystander*, 'At the centre of our being is a point of nothingness which is untouched by sin and illusion, a point of pure truth, a point or spark that belongs entirely to God.'[11] The heart of Merton's mystical philosophy is that *Esse est Deus* – God is eternal being, purity of being, the ground and cause of all things.

Spiritual freedom, love, commitment to the marginalised and ecumenism – these are the aspirations Merton had for his Church, a Church in touch with its entire people and its origins in Jesus. Bishop Monahan's book shows us how utterly important Merton remains today as a spiritual writer, a social activist and most importantly a true man of God. In today's troubled world, we need more than ever Merton's call to contemplation, silence and interiority and, above all, his understanding that we are all interconnected. Why do Thomas Merton's compelling writings continue to appeal to so many? I think that John O'Donohue provides the best answer:

Only holiness will call people to listen now. And the work of holiness is not about perfection or niceness; it is about belonging, that sense of being in the Presence and through the quality of that belonging, the mild magnetic of implicating others in the Presence. This is not about forging a relationship with a distant God but about the realisation that we are already within God.[12]

Dr Máire Áine Ní Mhainnín,
Lecturer in French, School of Languages,
Literatures and Cultures (French), NUI Galway

---

[1] Pope Francis, Address of the Holy Father to the Joint Session of the United States Congress, Washington, DC, 24 September 2015, http://www.vatican.va/content/francesco/en/speeches/2015/september/documents/papa-francesco_20150924_usa-us-congress.html
[2] *New Seeds of Contemplation*, p. 31.
[3] Matthew Fox, *Meister Eckhart: A Mystic-Warrior for Our Times*, California: New World Library, 2014, p. 281.
[4] 'The Nobleman' in *The Complete Mystical Works of Meister Eckhart*, M.O'C. Walshe (trans. and ed.), New York: Crossroad Publishing, 2009, p. 564; see also 'Sermon 4', p. 57.
[5] *The Courage for Truth*, p. 87.
[6] Jean Sulivan, 'Thomas Merton', *Le Monde*, 25 December 1970, https://www.lemonde.fr/archives/article/1970/12/25/thomas-merton_2642182_1819218.html
[7] *The Sign of Jonas*, p. 281.
[8] Reiner Schürmann, *Wandering Joy: Meister Eckhart's Mystical Philosophy*, MA: Lindisfarne Books, 2001, p. 18.
[9] *New Seeds of Contemplation*, p. 296–7.
[10] Thomas Aquinas, *Summa Contra Gentiles*, Book III, part I, A.C. Pegis (trans. and ed.), Indiana: University of Notre Dame Press, 1975, p. 224.
[11] *Conjectures of a Guilty Bystander*, p. 158.
[12] Quoted in Brene Brown, *Braving the Wilderness: The Quest for True Belonging and the Courage to Stand Alone*, Maine: Thorndike Press, 2018, p. 132.

Note on the Cover Portrait

The portrait of Thomas Merton is by Harry Guinnane, an Ennis-based artist. It is an engaging portrait with a great sense of presence. Its colours subtly suggest the many shades of Merton the man. The abstract background space allows the observer to engage fully with the subject and to be drawn to join Merton as a companion pilgrim.

Merton was not a vain man and he had a self-deprecatory sense of humour that endeared him to many. Jim Forest said that Merton had a face that reminded him of David Duncan's photos of Pablo Picasso, 'similarly unfettered in its expressiveness, the eyes bright and quick and sure, suggesting some strange balance between wisdom and mischief'. Forest goes on to say that Merton once remarked that his was the face of a 'hillbilly who knows where the still is'.[1]

Harry Guinnane spent time studying the eyes in order to get right their friendly, gregarious and yet penetrating nature. He also captures the hint of mischief – that sense of knowing 'where the still is'.

Merton's own view that good art can give insight into God is reflected in Harry's achievement in capturing in the outer eyes the suggestion of the insight and vision of the inner eye. Peace smiles in this portrait and evokes the lasting peace that is the smile of the beatific vision.

---

[1] Jim Forest, *Living with Wisdom: A Life of Thomas Merton*, New York: Orbis Books, 2008, p. xi.

Short Chronology of Thomas Merton's Life

1915	31 January, Born in Prades, France
1916	Moved to USA
1921	His mother, Ruth Merton, died
1928	Moved to England from France
1931	His father, Owen Merton, died
1933	Started at University of Cambridge
1934	Left Cambridge to return to the United States
1935	Started at Columbia University
1938	Graduated from Columbia University and began MA studies
1938	16 November, Received into the Catholic Church
1940	Taught English at St Bonaventure College
1941	10 December, Entered the Trappist Abbey of Gethsemani, Kentucky
1943	His brother, John Paul Merton, killed in WWII
1948	Published *The Seven Storey Mountain*
1949	Ordained a priest
1951	Master of Scholastics
1955	Master of Novices
1958	Fourth and Walnut epiphany in Louisville
1964	Interreligious dialogue in New York
1965	Living full time in the hermitage
1968	American and Asian tour
1968	10 December, Death by accidental electrocution

Introduction

> So much do I love this solitude that when I walk out along the road to the old barns that stand alone, far from the old buildings, delight begins to overpower me from head to foot and peace smiles even in the marrow of my bones.[1]

Thomas Merton is the most influential Christian spiritual thinker, writer and commentator to have lived in the twentieth century. He has crossed over to the twenty-first century still bearing those same credentials. People can be ambiguous in their approach to Merton: on the one hand acknowledging his great contribution and on the other hand they can almost dismiss him with a resigned sigh of 'Oh, well, Merton is Merton'. I am never quite sure what they mean, but I hazard a guess that when they first discovered Merton they found him inspiring, exciting and even life-changing. Then, somewhere along their life's journey, they went off Merton; he no longer spoke to them.

There is something about the delight that Thomas Merton felt in rambling around the grounds of his monastery's old buildings that speaks to my own sense of place and where I was when I first read about him. It was during my seminary days in Maynooth and I was reading his famed autobiography, *The Seven Storey Mountain*. I was deeply moved by the book, overpowered to some extent, and looking back on that happy memory, I can still feel a peace that smiles even in the marrow of my own bones.

Back then and ever since I have remained hooked on Merton. I have written before that I was drawn to the work of saints John Henry Newman, Augustine, Teresa of Ávila and

Thérèse of Lisieux alongside Thomas Merton as nurture for my own spiritual life. The immediate and compelling appeal of Thomas Merton was that he was more contemporary than those other giants of spirituality. Merton had lived in the century in which I was living and had only died in 1968, a few years before I started to read his work. Merton wrote in a language that was accessible with a literary flair and style that had its origins in pre- and post-war Europe and the United States. He spoke a language that was contemporary and had all the realism of the world in which I lived.

I have already placed him in the company of four saints and I would like to think that he too will be canonised someday. It is perhaps this contemporary edge that will delay canonisation in Merton's case. He wrote and spoke in the vernacular of modern times without the sometimes-archaic modes of expression associated with the older saints just mentioned. Somehow, I feel it will be a while before Merton will be declared a saint. I recall the theologian Mary T. Malone saying in a conference on Merton that for whatever reason the Church is never happy with the vernacular. There seems to be a safety of distance in people of the far-off past that is lacking in those of our time who speak our own language. Merton certainly spoke our language and in doing so created quite a following for himself, but equally he ruffled a lot of feathers and made enemies for himself. I recall one priest is alleged to have said of Merton's early and tragic death that maybe God had taken him before he could do any more harm to the Church.

Merton was an ants-in-your-pants kind of man. He was restless in his quest for solitude, challenging the monastic life for its failings; a hermit who refused to be trapped within the boundaries of his hermitage, he embraced the life of a celibate monk and he fell in love with a woman a short time before he died. He used language well, yet he struggled to find the language of silence. Part of Merton's attraction for me is that he is a man of contradictions. He shows us that one of the most powerful gifts in life is to change in order to grow in our understanding and self-development as a means of discovering Christ in ourselves – in the 'cell of the inner self'.[2] To read and study Merton is to be in great company, but he can be exhausting company too, which is probably part of the reason for some peoples' ambiguity towards him.

I invite you to come with me on a voyage to rediscover Thomas Merton. I will share with you my favourite Merton writings and I will take you through some of the uncharted waters that heretofore you might have hesitated to navigate on the grounds that you feared them to be too deep – Merton being Merton.

✠ Fintan Monahan

---

[1] *The Sign of Jonas*; quoted in Thomas P. McDonnell (ed.), *Through the Year with Thomas Merton: Daily Meditations from His Writings*, New York: Image Books, 1985, p. 48.

[2] John Eudes Bamberger, *Thomas Merton: Prophet of Renewal*, Minnesota: Liturgical Press, 2005, p. 123.

CHAPTER ONE

Merton's Early Years

Often it is to the birds or trees that he makes these pagan screams of joy.[1]

Thomas Merton was born on Sunday, 31 January 1915. There are many things about him that surprise people, beginning with the fact that he was not, as they might expect, born in either the United States of America or England, both of which are commonly mistaken as his birthplace.

A Place called Prades

He was born in Prades, a village in France near the border with Spain. It might be more surprising that his parents were not French. His father, Owen Merton, was from New Zealand and his mother, Ruth Jenkins, was a native of the United States. Ruth and Owen were artists, which may also surprise readers. I will drop the surprise theme now lest it become repetitive and boring, but be prepared for more.

Owen and Ruth met when they were art students in Paris in 1913. They fell in love and when their art tutor moved to England they moved there too and were married on 7 April 1914. Between them they had little money and Owen was determined not to take financial handouts from Ruth's father, who was prepared to assist them.

The couple moved back to France and set up home in an apartment in Prades, where Owen hoped to further his career as a watercolourist and make his name as an artist. Their son Thomas was born in Prades soon after their arrival there. Ruth insisted that he be called Tom not Thomas. She doted on him and kept a diary about his babyhood, which became known as 'Tom's Book'.

Neither of his parents was religious though they came from religious backgrounds (Ruth was Episcopalian and Owen Church of England) and the child Merton grew up without any formal religious education or practice. His mother imbued him with a sense of his own worth and regarded him from an early age as a prodigy of sorts. She writes:

> When he hears music he begins to dance, changing to fast or slow steps as the music changes. Sometimes when he is playing, he sings, but without much tune. When we go out he seems conscious of everything. Sometimes he puts up his arms and cries out 'Oh Sui! Oh Joli!' Often it is to the birds or trees that he makes these pagan screams of joy.[2]

Ruth may well be displaying signs of a mother who thinks her sons or daughters are swans as opposed to ducks or drakes, but her artistic temperament shows through in her words. I think the phrase 'pagan screams of joy' is her interpretation of what she saw as the little boy's already burgeoning artistic spirit.

The Importance of Place

Ruth was a freethinker and she wanted her child to grow up in a freethinking though disciplined atmosphere. She wanted her son to express himself intellectually and be so enabled by the artistic surrounds of the house and home. I deliberately distinguish between house and home because Ruth set great store on the sheer physicality of the dwelling and its role in the transformation of a house into a home.

Her artistic interest and skills lay in the field of interior design. She believed in the artistic arrangement and layout of a house. It was important to her that a house be artistically designed so as to influence those who lived there as well as creating a secure and happy environment for them. I imagine Ruth would be sympathetic to the popular feng shui movement of interior arrangement which harnesses the flow of positive energy (chi) in a house. This ancient Chinese belief is fashionable today among many people and is ridiculed by as many more. I feel that the most sceptical should be kind enough to admit that even if it doesn't do much good, it can't do any harm. I like to think that Ruth Merton's belief in the power of interior design planted the seed that was to grow into her son's interest in the spiritual call of the East much later in his life.

Ruth's emphasis on the 'space beautiful' also gave Tom a sense of the importance of places that lasted throughout his life. His mother made the home space a beautiful one that was comfortable and conducive to learning and creativity. Merton grew to always have a keen appreciation of places and he carried the memories of places with him at all times. It was as though every place he ever lived in or visited seemed to stay with him forever. He travelled to many places and in his memory those places travelled with him. It was a most valuable asset to him as a writer and it also gave him the ability to put down roots anywhere, be his stay long or short. Michael Mott, Merton's biographer, wrote, 'The importance of place in his life he clearly inherited from Ruth.'[3]

A Disrupted Childhood

Thomas Merton did not have an unhappy childhood but he had a disrupted one. He was cared for, loved, encouraged and made to have a sense of his own self-worth. Both parents believed in his ability and potential and wanted him to get the best out of himself. The first major disruption that occurred was as a result of the turmoil that was gripping Europe at the time because of World War I. For their safety the Merton family left France in 1916 and went to the United States. It was the beginning of the real relationship between young Tom and his maternal family, consisting of his grandfather, grandmother and Uncle Harold.

Whilst Ruth was happy to be with her own family on home ground, she was somewhat torn between them and her loyalty to her husband. Owen was still unwilling to accept financial assistance from his father-in-law and persisted in attempting to support Ruth and Tom by taking gardening work, playing piano in a cinema and of course hoping to sell his artworks.

In 1918 they had a second son, John Paul. Ruth continued to work hard at child-rearing, teaching Tom and keeping him to a strict learning regime. She continued to record his words and actions and she took to recording similar facts about John Paul. Ruth Merton comes across as a very loving mother who had ambitions for her children and these ambitions pointed towards the pursuit of matters intellectual in life.

It was a demanding time for Ruth whose husband at that stage did not seem to be as involved in the children's lives and was more taken up with his artistic career. Her health deteriorated and she was stricken with cancer of the stomach when Tom was almost four years old. She died in 1921 when he was six years old. Ruth's death was a catastrophic disruption of the entire Merton family's life. One does not need to have any training in psychology to realise the impact of a mother's death on a child of six. His mother's death created a lasting void in young Tom's life.

The circumstances leading to her death and subsequent funeral have been noted by Thomas Merton and commented on by the many who have studied his life and work. Ruth Merton died in hospital having not seen her son for the last few months of her life and hospitalisation. It seems to have been her choice and from today's perspective we might think it strange; however, it was (and in some cases still is) common practice to shield children from the reality of death and dying.

A Mother's Letter to her Son

What makes Ruth Merton's approach to her impending death unique is her decision to write a final letter to her young son. It says much about Ruth's almost obsessive ambition for him to be self-fulfilling in life that she wrote him a letter on her deathbed. Despite his tender years she felt that he would cope with such a letter. Was it tough love or a desire to spare him from seeing her wasted state in hospital that made her choose to take her leave of her son in a letter? We can only surmise, but Ruth's feelings at the time cannot be overlooked: she was coping with dying and its attendant personal traumas and she must have been heartbroken at the prospect of leaving her loved ones behind – her husband, children and her own parents and sibling.

It required a unique, if misguided, courage for Ruth to pen that final letter to her son. There may be differing views as she was known to be headstrong and prone to make unusual decisions and in particular she liked to be at variance with popular opinion. The contents of the letter are unknown apart from the fact that it informed Tom that she was dying and that they would not meet again. The letter's contents and the notion of such a letter make us stop and think. It is not for us to suggest that he was emotionally scarred by these events but from today's perspective with its advances in child-psychology we can assume that the run-up to his mother's death and her funeral made a lasting impression on Merton.

After Ruth's death his father, Owen, left Tom with his maternal grandparents and devoted time to his art. It was not a case of his abandoning Tom but rather a case of a thoughtless disregard for the boy's immediate need of a father – his only remaining parent. The second son, John Paul, aged three, was also left in grandparental care.

Owen Merton struggled with his relationship with his wife's family, and yet he was happy to avail of their willingness to act as surrogate parents for his children. Perhaps he needed time to come to terms with his own loss as well as devoting more time to his art. By 1925 he had reasserted himself as the parent in charge by leaving for France and taking Tom with him. He left John Paul in the care of Ruth's parents.

Formal Education Begins

In France the Merton father and son settled once more near Prades. Tom's early education in France consisted of boarding in a *lycée* in Montauban and his father set up home in Saint-Antonin and sought to further his career as an artist. Tom was not happy in his new school and experienced some bullying. Gradually he settled in and he did well in his studies without showing exemplary abilities. He, along with a few friends, wrote little novels – a sign of the budding writer.

In June 1928 they returned to England to further Owen's career as a painter; however, Owen became ill and subsequently died in England of a brain tumour on 18 January 1931. Once more Tom's childhood was disrupted by family tragedy and, as with his mother's death, the loss of his father made a lasting impact on Tom, who at this point in his life was an adolescent of sixteen.

It is here that I choose to end this section on Merton's early years simply in order to emphasise my point that up to his sixteenth year a lot of emotional trauma had befallen the child, the boy and the adolescent Merton. These traumas decided the course of action that Merton took from then on, including his conversion to Catholicism in 1938 and his eventual entry into the monastery in 1941. In the next section I will address the adult Merton's life, mindful of the influence of events up to his sixteenth year.

---

[1] Ruth Merton, *Tom's Book: To Granny with Tom's Best Love 1916*, Sheila Milton (ed.), Monterey, KY: Larkspur Press, 2005 (1 November 1916); quoted in Michael Mott, *The Seven Mountains of Thomas Merton*, Boston: Houghton Mifflin, 1984, p. 688.

[2] Ibid.

[3] Mott, *The Seven Mountains of Thomas Merton*, p. 205.

CHAPTER TWO

Becoming a Catholic and Embracing a Life of Solitude

I had to be led by a way that I could not understand, and I had to follow a path that was beyond my own choosing.[1]

The previous chapter ended with Thomas Merton aged sixteen orphaned by the death of his father from a tumour of the brain. He was orphaned but not alone in the world. His brother was at this time still living with their maternal grandparents in the United States. Thomas Merton was not alone in his parentless life. The void created by the loss of his parents, while never emotionally filled, was to some extent cushioned by material circumstances. Firstly, he had the support of his godfather, Tom Bennet, his father's friend and Tom's designated mentor-guardian, who with his wife tried to keep a parental eye out for him. Also, his maternal grandparents were anxious that he come to live with them in the United States. It was agreed that first he should finish his education in England. He studied for two more years at Oakham boarding school, where he had been since 1930. He then went on to Cambridge University to study literature in 1933. His grandfather settled an annual allowance on him that made his living situation more comfortable.

The Cambridge Year

Thomas Merton, aged eighteen, began his university life with a promising future ahead of him if his intellect was anything to go by. There was talk of a possible career in the diplomatic corps after university.

In *The Seven Storey Mountain*, Merton's account of his time in Cambridge paints an unhappy picture of a time and place full of moral degeneration and sinfulness to which he the callow youth succumbed with the appetite of a great sinner. The Catholic convert and aspirant monk-writer seems determined to portray his short time in Cambridge as a debauched life in an equally debauched setting. He wrote of Cambridge:

> some people might live there for three years, or even a lifetime, so protected that they never sense the sweet stench of corruption that is all around them – the keen, thick scent of decay that pervades everything and accuses with a terrible accusation the superficial youthfulness, the abounding undergraduate noise that fills those ancient buildings. But for me with my blind appetites, it was impossible that I should not rush in and take a huge bite of this rotten fruit. The bitter taste is still with me after not a few years.[2]

Merton's memory of his time in Cambridge was painful and his writing about it some fifteen years later reflects the anger, bitterness, sense of failure that he had towards his behaviour at the age of eighteen. At the time of writing about Cambridge it is clear that he still had unresolved personal issues about his life back then.

It is interesting that he seems unable to confront those issues head-on and instead he, a man of thirty-three, reverts to being the confused eighteen-year-old and seeks to pin blame on the very institution of Cambridge itself. There is something juvenile in this and one can only surmise that he was somewhat in denial about the truth of that misspent year. In effect, however, that is all it was – one year in his life, the type of year often excused as the sowing of one's wild oats. There is a sense in his writing that he would rather wish it all away, acknowledge it briefly and learn to live with his regrets. It is important to remember, too, that Merton's writing was being vetted by Community censors, who perhaps curtailed his openness and full disclosure of his past.

What was so dramatic about that year that he chose to write of it with such revulsion – sweet stench of corruption, the all-pervading sense of decay and the superficiality of youth, the blind appetites indulging in all the rottenness – just what is he talking about?

There is no denying that at eighteen Merton was more a man of the world than the average student arriving in his first year at Cambridge. He had returned from a summer on the continent where he had lived it up in terms of wine, women and song. He arrived in Cambridge and continued to live a similar lifestyle. He stood out as a young man who liked to revel at the expense of his studies and generally get by on his reputation as an intellectual. Before long he paid a price for his over-indulgence. It culminated in his fathering a child with a girlfriend and this scandal was the reason that he was removed from Cambridge and his godfather unceremoniously sent him back to the United States from England.

Little is known about either the woman or their child, a boy, and it is said that both died in London during The Blitz (1940–1). Tom Bennett ensured that a financial arrangement be put in place for the support of the mother and child and is said to have promised Merton not to tell his grandparents about the incident if he agreed to leave England and not return to study in Cambridge. There is no doubt that Merton lived with guilt about this throughout his life, but guilt a victim does not make and our admiration for the man he became in later life should not diminish the fact that the mother and their child were victims too.

Of course, we should acknowledge the recklessness of youth and be understanding and, above all, forgiving of past actions, but never excuse on the grounds of youth and inexperience alone. At the same time, it must be said that this was the 1930s and society had a long way to go before having a child out of wedlock would be seen as anything but a scandal of disastrous proportions, for the woman and for the man. The latter, as history proves, often avoids the consequences by turning his back and walking away into the shadow of anonymity. Merton's behaviour was typical of the time, and would remain so for many years to come – he was not unlike many of his male peers then and since.

Steadying Influences

A more chastened Merton returned to the States, where he reunited with his brother John Paul and his late mother's family. He hadn't lost his appetite for life, but he did begin to take his studies seriously and he read a lot. He enrolled at Columbia University to study English literature, and went on to write a postgraduate thesis on the poetry and art of William Blake.

It was at Columbia that he met a group of fellow students that were to become lifelong friends. He stood out among this group as leader, hellraiser (he hadn't totally reformed), and a sharp intuitive debater on the big and small questions of life.

One of the big questions that had long haunted him became, during his time at Columbia, more intense – the question of God, personal faith and religious affiliation. Merton, like his group of friends, was at an age when the quest for meaning in life was uppermost in his mind. The shadow of World War II loomed on the horizon, and it acutely focused their thinking. Merton felt the winds of change blowing in his own interior life and before long those winds caused him to drift towards the Catholic Church as the safe harbour in which the true meaning of life lay.

Soon after his birth Merton had been baptised into the Anglican tradition, the Church of England to which his father belonged. Formal religion did not play a large part in his or his parents' lives. Yet, they were creative people with a sense that their art expressed their interior feelings, so one could say that they were people with a spiritual sense. This was something they passed on to Thomas in his genes and in the atmosphere in which he was reared. He grew up to be an agnostic in his late teens and early adulthood. He does not seem to have had a strong antipathy to religion, but as he said himself after a serious bout of blood poisoning:

The thought of God, the thought of prayer did not even enter my mind, either that day, or all the rest of the time that I was ill, or that whole year. Or if the thought did come to me, it was only as an occasion for its denial and rejection.[3]

It would be wrong to imply that Merton's conversion to Catholicism was a sudden on-the-road-to-Damascus style conversion. In effect, Merton's drift in that direction took place over a period of five years from the start of his days in Columbia University (1933) and took a more definite direction around 1938 when he was teaching English in the Franciscan-run St Bonaventure College.

Becoming a Catholic

There is a famous incident recorded in *The Seven Storey Mountain* in which Merton and his friend Robert Lax are walking down Sixth Avenue in New York discussing their future lives. Lax asks Merton what he wants to be and he answers that in his heart he desires above all else to become a good Catholic. Lax replies that it is not sufficient to say he wants to be a good Catholic but that he should want and aspire to be a saint. Lax was a Jew with a deep sense of God in his life. He was someone Merton admired and regarded as truly good, genuine and God-loving. Somehow, having Lax suggest personal sainthood as a goal in life did not seem either flippant or jocose, but something to be deeply considered and borne in mind. Merton from that point on lived life with the desire for sainthood.

This did not mean that Merton had an ambition to be a canonised saint (such an ambition would surely be self-defeating and contradictory), but rather believed that we should all be motivated by sainthood and that it is the ultimate calling of every Christian to live a life aspiring to such perfection. Sainthood was Merton's kindly light in the darkness of life that led him at first to the Catholic Church and in time to the monastic life.

He was received into the Catholic Church on 16 November 1938. He wrote in his journals some ten years later recalling his baptism and the direction his life took from that moment on: 'Now, at last, let me begin to live by faith. Seek first, therefore, the kingdom of God.'[4] This sense of his life as a continuous unfolding of his Catholic faith is a recurring theme in Merton's writing. It meant so much to him to feel that he was now adorned with a faith that brought direction, grace and hope to his heretofore empty life. Becoming a Catholic was everything to Thomas Merton.

The Draw of the Monastery

Meaning had come into his life, but the search for the deeper meaning within the meaning continued. Merton lived a very full life for the following years: he wrote, he partied and was the life and soul of gatherings in a mixed company of friends. Yet, he hankered after something more fulfilling and began to explore the possibilities of becoming a priest. He approached the Franciscan Order and initially they were receptive to the idea of his joining, but in time they turned down his application once they discovered the worldlier baggage Merton would be bringing with him. On being told by his friend Dan Walsh (who had also recommended the Franciscans) about a retreat he had made at the Trappist Abbey of Gethsemani near Bardstown, Kentucky, Merton decided to go on a similar retreat in Holy Week 1941.

Pax Intrantibus ('Peace to those who enter') was the welcoming sign over the monastery's entrance and on passing through this hallowed portal Merton felt he had arrived in more senses than one:

> Everything I wanted to do the most, I can now try to do all the time without any interference ... As soon as I got inside, I knew I was home, where I never had been or would be a stranger.[5]

In December of that same year, he returned to Gethsemani and was admitted as a postulant choir monk. He was given the name Br Mary Louis and after ordination in 1949 he was known as Fr Louis.

A Different World

From 1941 to his death in 1968 – just over half his lifetime – Merton was a monk of Gethsemani. In effect, Merton spent half of his life in the secular world and half the religious world of the monastery. People tend to overlook the fact that twenty-seven years, from 1941 to 1968, is a long time and that Merton spent much of that time in the relative obscurity of the monastic life. From the publication of *The Seven Storey Mountain* in 1948, however, the anonymity guaranteed by the monastic enclosure quickly disappeared and Fr Louis became well known as Thomas Merton, monk, writer and artist. Yet he still lived in the monastery and abided by its strict rules and observances. This was an austere and severe life that to the outsider seems at once too difficult to handle and endlessly fascinating.

Abbot Richard Purcell of Mount Melleray Abbey describes the Trappists as 'hermits in community'. The punishing routine or *horarium* of the day never ceases to intrigue me, especially the early rising in the small hours of the morning. I shudder to think of the Chapter of Faults, a meeting of the members of the community in which any infringements of the Rule were publicly confessed; humiliating to say the least, but such was the intention. The rules concerning clothing and bathing might also offend our modern sensibilities: 'Underclothing was changed once a week in summer, once every two weeks in winter, showers and baths were virtually unknown.'[6]

This was the way of life Merton readily embraced and adhered to for twenty-seven years. It was a world with its own unique customs and traditions that allowed the monk to empty himself of the taints of the outside world and live a life devoted to God and with a constant eye on the end life as the ultimate goal. Life in the monastery was so focused on eternity that it was the accepted monastic tradition to greet the death of a monk with joy. In his writings, Thomas Merton not only embraced but extolled that path of austerity as represented by the monastic calling.

The Call of Two Worlds

After the success of *The Seven Storey Mountain*, Merton not only began a busy life of writing, but he engaged more and more with the world outside the monastery. He engaged in correspondence with a variety of people from the Russian novelist Boris Pasternak to Daniel Berrigan and the Dali Lama. He became involved with issues of racism, peace and the other prevailing issues of the late 1950s and into the 1960s. He still maintained his quest for inner peace and solitude within the monastery. He showed himself to be a constant searcher for inner truth and his opinions and interests shifted with every new encounter, whether it was in his studies, prayer or simply meeting old and new friends. He was a man of two worlds but always more at home in the monastic world.

Critics

Jim Forest in *Living with Wisdom: A Life of Thomas Merton* has a terse line that reads, 'Yet Merton is not without his critics.'[7] It is a line that speaks volumes and it would be naive to say that Merton was beyond reproach. Time and again, his critics call him a freelancer, someone who wanted the best of both worlds (secular and monastic), and all in all an egocentric and even egomaniacal figure. Naturally, I am not a harsh critic of Merton, but that is not to say that I do not accept his faults and his many weaknesses, for faults and weaknesses are part and parcel of all humanity.

A major failing often identified by the anti-Merton faction is his love affair with a young nurse named Margie whom he met while in hospital with back pain in March 1966. Their relationship lasted throughout the summer months and it brought great joy to Merton, while at the same time testing his commitment to the religious life. The prevailing judgement at the time would have been to blame the woman as the Eve who tempted this good and unsuspecting Adam; however, Merton was nothing but accepting of his active role in their relationship. Finally, it came to the attention of his Abbot who, while being kind to Merton, made it perfectly clear that it was either the monastery or his lover.

Merton made the choice to remain in the monastic life; however, he found it difficult to break ties with his beloved and they continued to meet occasionally (in secret) until October of 1966. Merton wrote with feeling about his love for Margie and her reciprocal love of him. Margie maintained a lifetime of silence about her relationship with Merton. It is not my purpose to make any judgement on Merton's love affair but simply to acknowledge it and that, by his account, both were genuinely in love. It would be verging on the prurient to give it any more attention.

Looking East

Towards the end, Merton's life had taken a new direction. His interest in exploring the riches of Eastern religious traditions brought him, in 1968, on an Asian tour, his first international journey since entering the monastery. He wrote even then that his ties with Gethsemani would never be broken:

> I suppose I ought eventually to end my days there. I do in many ways miss it. There is no problem of my wanting simply to 'leave Gethsemani'. It is my monastery and being away has helped me see it in perspective and love it more.[8]

On 10 December 1968 he delivered an address to an international religious conference in Bangkok. He left the lecture room to go to his bedroom, where he showered and was fatally electrocuted when a faulty electric fan fell on him.

The sudden and abrupt ending of Thomas Merton's life by accidental electrocution is the apotheosis of the Trappist calling brought home to us in stark reality. It was as though his vow of stability to the monastic state and place was calling him home – home to Gethsemani and the home to which every monk directed his life – the eternal home.

Merton had made himself a thorn in the side of the US political establishment by his anti-nuclear and anti-racist stance. Latterly, his opposition to the Vietnam War made him stand out even more as being non-government-friendly.

Because of this conspiracy theorists were convinced that his death was not accidental, but that he was murdered by forces or agents of the US government. No concrete evidence has ever emerged to substantiate such a claim; but the assassinations of Senator Robert F. Kennedy and Martin Luther King Jr in the same year fuelled the spread of the conspiracy theory.

Merton's tragic death in a foreign land and the return of his body a week later for burial in the grounds of Gethsemani was a test of that community's tradition of joy at the death of a brother monk. Merton was certainly an exception to many rules of this life, and one senses the sadness of his community at his passing even though no one begrudged him his eternal homecoming to God whom he loved above all else.

The words of his abbot, Dom Flavian Burns, in a homily to the community sum up the mixed feelings of joy and sadness at Merton's leaving them in death. His words are not only apt but also deeply inspiring:

> The world knew him from his books: we knew him from his spoken word. Few, if any, know him in his secret prayer. Still, he had a secret prayer, and this is what gave the inner life to all he said and wrote. His secret was his secret to himself to a great extent, but he was a skilful reader of the secret of the souls that sought his help. It is because of this that although we laughed at him, and with him, as we would a younger brother, still we respected him as the spiritual father of our souls.[9]

---

[1] *The Seven Storey Mountain*; quoted in Jim Forest, *Living with Wisdom: A Life of Thomas Merton*, New York: Orbis Books, 2008, p. 71.

[2] *The Seven Storey Mountain*, p. 118.

[3] *The Seven Storey Mountain*, p. 108.

[4] Merton recalls his baptism in his journal, 16 November 1957; quoted in *The Sign of Jonas*.

[5] *The Sign of Jonas*; quoted in Forest, *Living with Wisdom*, p. 85.

[6] M. Basil Pennington, *Thomas Merton, Brother Monk: The Quest for True Freedom*, San Francisco: Harper and Row, 1987, p. 3.

[7] Forest, *Living with Wisdom*, p. 242.

[8] *The Asian Journal*; quoted in Mary Gordon, *On Thomas Merton*, Boulder: Shambhala, 2018, p. 111.

[9] Dom Flavian's homily; quoted in Forest, *Living with Wisdom*, p. 239.

CHAPTER THREE

The Seven Storey Mountain

And everybody calmly tells me:
writing is your vocation.[1]

Most people who know anything about Thomas Merton will have come to that knowledge through his famous autobiography, *The Seven Storey Mountain*. Merton wrote it at the age of thirty-one, five years after entering the monastery at Gethsemani. In the book, Merton tells the story from his birth in 1915 up to his early days in the monastery. It is a beautifully written testament of an intensely active and brilliant young man, who led a full and worldly life and who in relatively young adulthood turned his back on that life, converted to Catholicism and entered a monastery that practised one of the most austere and ascetic forms of monastic life.

Outstanding Titles
Either Merton or his publisher had an eye for unusual and curiously apt titles. *The Seven Storey Mountain* is one example, but there are many throughout his writing career, in which he wrote some fifty books, including: *The Seven Storey Mountain*; *The Sign of Jonas*; *Conjectures of a Guilty Bystander*; *The Waters of Siloe*; *The Ascent to Truth*; *Bread in the Wilderness*; *New Seeds of Contemplation*; *Mystics and Zen Masters*.

The Seven Storey Mountain remains his signature work and is often referred to as being in the company of St Augustine's *Confessions* and John Henry Newman's *Apologia Pro Vita Sua*. Before proceeding any further, it is fitting to do an exploration of the depth of meaning behind the title *The Seven Storey Mountain*.

The title is taken from the long narrative poem *Divine Comedy* by the Italian Dante Alighieri (1265–1321). In the poem, Dante is a pilgrim on a journey from hell through purgatory to heaven. He is guided on his way by Virgil (who represents human reason), Beatrice (who represents divine revelation) and St Bernard of Clairvaux (who represents contemplative mysticism and devotion to Mary).

Having survived the depths of hell, Dante and Virgil ascend from the underworld to the Mountain of Purgatory on the far side of the world. The mountain has seven terraces, corresponding to the seven deadly sins or the 'seven roots of sinfulness'. The seven-tiered mountain is the symbol of the modern world and the struggles and battles to avoid evil and do good in order to reach the goal of heaven. The seven purgatorial steps on the mountain of this world include Pride, Envy, Wrath, Sloth, Avarice, Gluttony and Lust.

Dante's great poem speaks not only to his own time, but it has continued to speak to humankind's struggle with good and evil ever since. The graphic language of the poem would have captivated Merton the poet and artist. It would have matched his love for the riches of Italian church art, a love affair that began when he was a youth of sixteen on a visit to Rome.

However, the narrative outline of the poem – one man escaping from hell, enduring purgatory and attaining heaven – was what really spoke to Merton at that time in his life. He felt his life to date had been a mirror image of the Divine Comedy: a hell and a purgatory on earth and monastic life was the way for him to climb the seven tiers (storeys) to heaven.

Ascending the Mountain

The monastic life that Merton had chosen for himself was austere and demanded strict obedience to the monastery's abbot or superior. Merton's first abbot in Gethsemani was Dom Frederic Dunne, the son of a bookbinder. This was, in Merton's eyes, a mixed blessing. On entering the monastery, he was prepared to sacrifice his great passion for writing. It was part of the 'new' man and a new life devoted entirely to

God. Dom Frederic recognised and appreciated Merton's literary talent and encouraged him from the outset to continue his writing in whatever form he chose – be it poetry or prose. It came as a surprise to Merton, who had assumed that writing would be forbidden, that he was instead bound by obedience to write.

In March of 1946, Merton's revelation to his confessor that he was interested in writing his own life story was greeted with laughter; however, the Abbot felt it was a good idea and encouraged him greatly. Despite his own desire to write and the encouragement of the Abbot, Merton had qualms about the project. He feared that it would be regarded as an ego trip for someone so young to write his life story. His main reluctance was his feeling that it might distract him from giving himself fully to his true calling, a life of prayer as a Trappist monk.

GK Chesterton, whose famous autobiography was published in 1936, had been laughed at for writing his own life story. Merton would never have imagined though that he would become as well known as Chesterton, if not even better known. In any case Merton the monk, already vowed and bound to obedience, bowed his head and commenced writing his autobiography. Before long, a serious literary opus emerged, which *Time* magazine would later describe as having 'redefined the image of monasticism and made the concept of saintliness accessible to moderns'.[2]

In October 1946 the early manuscripts were sent to the publisher and it was accepted before the end of the year, but much to Merton's annoyance he ran into a bit of trouble within his order in the following spring. Apart from the accounts of his wild youth, one of the order's censors was less than impressed with Merton's writing style and felt he could do with a correspondence course in English grammar before writing any further books. Merton persevered and climbed on regardless of any such petty criticism (even though he readily accepted the role of the order's censors as part and parcel of a life committed to obedience) and the book was published early in 1948.

Reception

Initially, it appeared that there was going to be a disappointing lack of critical attention given to the book even though expectations were that it would be moderately successful. Suddenly, and there is no other way to put it, the book took off. Over six hundred thousand of the original cloth edition had sold by the end of 1948. This was a phenomenal sales record for any bestseller and especially this kind of book. Its popularity took everyone by surprise, not least Merton.

Some enthusiastic critics likened it to Augustine's *Confessions* and Newman's *Apologia Pro Vita Sua*, although it was also commented that it lacked the profundity of the former and the elegance of the latter. Merton's work in comparison to either of the other two might be described as a diamond in the rough.

It continues to sell well to this day and was included on the *National Review* list of the one hundred best non-fiction books of the twentieth century. It was also mentioned in *100 Christian Books That Changed the Century* (2000) by William J. Petersen.

Accounting for Success

Simply put, *The Seven Storey Mountain* is an extraordinary story told by a writer whose clear literary style allowed the story to flow. The timing of the book's publication was just right as it was released into a world that was badly in need of such a book. Its language was contemporary and appealed to a wide readership that in post-war America was looking for something different and meaningful. It came at that critical and challenging time of confusion, anger, disgust and soul-searching that had built up in the immediate aftermath of war. People were searching for meaning, looking for answers in the midst of chaos and Merton's book offered them new and deep spiritual pathways.

It is this appeal to the seeker of meaning that makes *The Seven Storey Mountain* popular with today's readership too. It appealed to a war-weary world when it first appeared and it appeals still to those who today for one reason or another are world-weary. It is an account of the honest and truthful quest of a modern person for meaning to life. Merton's autobiography remains relevant to a modern readership and its unequivocal answer to humankind's questions on truth, freedom and peace remains the same – it can only be found in God.

Jim Forest, who knew Merton and wrote a book about him, said of the success of *The Seven Storey Mountain*:

> Partly it is because the book is a massive love letter, the ultimate object of his devotion being God and all that God has given us for our good and salvation. Merton communicated a contagious enthusiasm for the life of faith, voluntary poverty, penance, and prayer. *The Seven Storey Mountain* remains an electrifying challenge to the idea that human happiness consists mainly of a proper diet, a good job, money in the bank, a comfortable address, and an active sex life.[3]

A Picture of Merton

Much of the biographical detail of *The Seven Storey Mountain* is dealt with in chapters one and two. The detail of Merton's early years, his family, school and literary interests is portrayed in *The Seven Storey Mountain* in an honest, open manner that takes the reader on an inner pilgrimage. The older Merton that emerges from *The Seven Storey Mountain* is a highly intellectual man with a passion for writing and the liberal arts in general. If Merton had never entered a monastery, he would probably have stayed a university lecturer, developed his writing and nurtured a keen interest in the very same social issues of peace, human rights and racism with which he engaged from his monastic setting.

Merton wanted more from life and in *The Seven Storey Mountain* he reflects on his early life and on the quest for faith in God that led to his conversion to Roman Catholicism at the age of twenty-three. Four years later Merton left behind a promising literary career, teaching English literature at St Bonaventure College, and entered the Trappist Abbey of

Gethsemani in Kentucky. He describes this transition as an entry into a 'new freedom', which he later described in *The Sign of Jonas* as a 'peace that smiles'. The inscription on the entry into Gethsemani monastery happens to be *Pax Intrantibus*, 'Peace to all who enter'. Merton found peace there, but it was a peace that encompassed much inner turmoil, questioning, seeking and conflict. For some, these may contradict the very notion of peace, but in Merton's case they authenticated the peace he sought and made his lifetime's goal and ambition that perfect peace of which St John Henry Newman speaks.[4]

Merton comes across as a fun-loving, gregarious extrovert, extraordinarily energetic and a good companion, a man who lived life with a degree of intensity for anything he put his active mind to.

The Seven Storey Burden

The book has its shortcomings. It is written in the fresh, energetic voice of a young man with all the zeal and focus of a convert. It has the forthrightness and righteousness of youth and, as such, can come across as judgemental in places. It falls into the trap of preachiness on occasion. Throughout there are glimpses of snobbery towards other groups within Christianity: somewhat sarcastic jabs are taken at non-Catholic Christianity; and there is an air of condescension when describing Catholic religious communities that less rigorous than the Trappists.

Today's readers will find that the writing style in places is quite of its time and some of the social issues of the time may seem light years away from where we are at present. Yet one senses that underlying issues of justice and peace are as relevant to us today as they were in Merton's time. The language too is characteristic of the time and suffers from a lack of inclusivity. Despite these issues, the fact remains that the work continues to sell well and inspire many, and that speaks for itself.

Later in life Merton was dismayed at how narrow and judgemental he had been and claimed that the author of *The*

Seven Storey Mountain was long dead and buried. By then, Merton's perspectives on his work in *The Seven Storey Mountain* had changed. In *The Sign of Jonas*, published in 1953, Merton says, '*The Seven Storey Mountain* is the work of a man I have never even heard of.'[5]

Merton penned an introduction to a 1966 Japanese edition of *The Seven Storey Mountain* and said:

> Perhaps if I were to attempt this book today, it would be written differently. Who knows? But it was written when I was still quite young, and that is the way it remains. The story no longer belongs to me.

This was not Merton disowning the book, but he had moved on and gained perspective on life and writing. At that point in his writing career, Merton was still experimenting with his literary style and skills. Evelyn Waugh, a prolific writer and Catholic convert, encouraged Merton and critiqued his writing. Waugh had edited the English edition of *The Seven Storey Mountain*, which appeared as *Elected Silence*. Waugh was a fine writer of perception and great sensibilities; he may well have found the forthrightness of Merton's style to be at times overbearing. Waugh toned down Merton's references to life in Cambridge for the English edition.

Waugh was steeped in the traditionalism of his Catholic faith. Merton too showed signs of the traditionalist bent sometimes associated with converts. It is a form of possessiveness that opposes any change to the system whose structure attracted them in the first instance. He liked the singing of the Psalms in the monastic prayer-routine and the attention to rubrical detail focused the mind; however, as time went on and with the advent of Vatican II, Merton saw that adherence to outward rules did not necessarily result in quality of worship. Waugh, I suspect, was intransigent when it came to interfering with matters such as the use of Latin in the Catholic Liturgy.

Waugh, despite any reservations he may have had, described *The Seven Storey Mountain* as, 'A book which may well prove to be of permanent interest in the history of religious experience.'[6] It has been said of Waugh's influence on Merton's work that he brought precision bombing in place of pattern bombing and that he tackled Merton on the exaggerations to which he was prone.[7]

Merton had worried over the style of his writing and in the run-up to writing and publishing *The Seven Storey Mountain* he had reread the work of John Henry Newman and decided that the style employed to great effect by Newman was not for him. He had always resisted refinement, just as he resisted Chesterton's chatty and urbane style. That was Merton's way.[8]

Enduring Legacy

Despite the book's weaknesses and Merton's own reservations, *The Seven Storey Mountain* remains an iconic masterpiece. It is, according to Jim Forest, 'one of the most compelling autobiographies ever written'.[9]

Its strengths easily outweigh its weaknesses and it was admired by many notable people. Recently, while discussing Merton, Bishop Robert Barron quotes Fulton Sheen, saying, 'The autobiography of Thomas Merton is a twentieth century form of the *Confessions* of St Augustine.[10] The novelist Graham Greene described it as, 'An autobiography with a pattern and meaning valid for all of us.'[11] Clare Boothe Luce, congresswoman, playwright, women's advocate and once managing editor of *Vanity Fair*, who was in regular correspondence with Merton, commented, 'It is to a book like this that men will turn a hundred years from now to find out what went on in the heart of man in this cruel century.'[12]

The closing line of *The Seven Storey Mountain* ends by admonishing the reader to 'learn to know the Christ of the burnt men'. It is ironic that Merton's death in 1968 was caused by accidental electrocution.

The Seven Storey Mountain propelled Merton into a life of paradoxes: a man who left a refined intellectual career for a labour-oriented rural existence, only to be led back into the realm of international opinion and debate; a man who spurned the literary world for the anonymity of Trappist monastic life, only to become a world-famous author; he wrote of his conviction of the importance of monasticism and he professed his devotion to remain fixed in the confines of a monastic cell, yet he yearned to travel throughout Asia. *The Seven Storey Mountain* was the springboard for his interesting and exciting journey that has edified the spiritual lives of many.

Despite its flaws, I have no hesitation in recommending *The Seven Storey Mountain* if one were to read just one Merton book. I still remember being enthused and enthralled by it as a young seminarian. It is the book of a lifetime, and yet Merton went on to write even better works. I love some of his later work on prayer and contemplation and particularly his simple work on St Bernard of Clairvaux, *The Last of the Fathers.* Yet, there is no escaping the appeal of *The Seven Storey Mountain*, which encapsulates so much of Merton the young man and his evolutionary path to greatness: the genuineness of his love of God, his struggles, his earnest seeking, his humour and above all else his raw honesty. Merton and his struggles as a young man held an appeal for his generation, similar to the secular appeal of the character of Holden Caulfield in JD Salinger's seminal novel *Catcher in the Rye*, published a few years later in 1951. Salinger may have written from experience, but Merton's lasting appeal is that he was a real man who throughout his life continued to grapple with the struggles of life. This real humanity of Merton is what sums up for me the lasting appeal of *The Seven Storey Mountain*.

When the Irish philosopher, author, poet, neighbour and friend John O'Donohue died in 2008 (at around the same age as Merton) we were left to speculate about what such a talented and visionary writer would have achieved if he had lived longer. The same can be said of Thomas Merton. I have no doubt that he would have made many more physical, mental and spiritual journeys into and out of the life of prayer and solitude – trips back and forth between the hermitage of Gethsemani and other places where wise people nurtured their wisdom and were open to mutual sharing of and learning more about that wisdom.

Many Jesuits do the Spiritual Exercises of St Ignatius of Loyola on a formal basis twice in their lifetimes. The first time is normally when they are approaching a time of critical discernment in deciding whether they should persist in their vocation. The second time is often around mid-life, when they have a time to reflect, look back on years lived in ministry and evaluate what is worth focusing on for their remaining years of service. I can only imagine how rich the reflection must be the second time round.

Similarly, for a man who wrote an autobiography at such a young age, I can only imagine what a second autobiography might have been like had Merton lived and had time to harvest a lifetime of monastic life, deep prayer and contemplation, considering the extraordinary depth of reading and insightful exploration this giant of a mind was capable of. I speculate that the original seven would have been exceeded by the addition of many more storeys. In the final words of *The Seven Storey Mountain* we get a hint that the journey to the top of the mountain, and hence the storey count, is never complete:

> *Sit finis libri, non finis quaerendi.*
> This may be the end of the book, but not the end of the search or quest.

Such words are immortal and we should take them to ourselves as the compass by which we navigate the voyage of our own lives of faith.

---

[1] 'Meditatio Pauperis in Solitudine', *The Seven Storey Mountain*, p. 410.
[2] 'Religion: The Mountain', *Time*, 11 April 1949,
http://content.time.com/time/magazine/article/0,9171,800091,00.html/
[3] Jim Forest, *Living with Wisdom: A Life of Thomas Merton*, New York: Orbis Books, 2008, p. 97.
[4] Fintan Monahan, *A Perfect Peace: Newman, Saint for Our Time*, Dublin: Veritas Publications, 2019, p. 33.
[5] *The Sign of Jonas*, p. 328.

[6] Quoted on the back cover of *The Seven Storey Mountain*, SPCK Classics, London: SPCK, 1990.

[7] See Mary Frances Coady, *Merton and Waugh: A Monk, A Crusty Old Man, and The Seven Story Mountain*, MA: Paraclete Press, 2015.

[8] Michael Mott, *The Seven Mountains of Thomas Merton*, Boston: Houghton Mifflin, 1984, p. 249.

[9] Forest, *Living with Wisdom*, p. 98.

[10] 'Bishop Baron on Thomas Merton, Spiritual Master', YouTube, https://youtu.be/5X8fp2CvQmA

[11] *The Seven Storey Mountain*, SPCK Classics, 1990.

[12] Ibid.

CHAPTER FOUR

Merton the Artist

It is a most recollected small painting.[1]

Reader, I would like you to imagine that we are in Thomas Merton's hermitage in Gethsemani and we are about to view a small painting that hangs there. It was gifted to Merton in the late 1950s by his friend, renowned American artist Ad Reinhardt. The painting is sometimes called 'The Black Cross'.

Looking at the painting, there is no obvious symbol of a cross or any covert religious symbol. All we see at first glance is a small canvas painted entirely black. Perhaps on closer look you will see a deeper shade of black running in a wide line across the middle of the painting. Now, look again and you will see two black rectangles, one on the bottom and top of the painting. You might think to yourself that when joined to the middle line the rectangles make up the shape of a cross, maybe, but in the main you see only black.

If you have the temerity to turn the painting around, you will see inscribed on the back the word 'Top' in plain print on the upper part of the canvas with an arrow pointing upwards, which must be the artist's indication of which way the painting must be hung in order to be viewed correctly. On the left-hand side of the wooden frame is the date 1957 and on the right are the words, 'Small Painting'. On the top of the panel of the frame is a dedication, 'For TM', and on the bottom panel is the artist's signature.

Merton's Response
The above is all the information we receive about the painting and it is far from illuminating, but Reinhardt was a painter

who did not believe in explaining or enlightening the viewer in any way. Looking at the front again, it has not changed; you see only black. You may be thinking that it is one of those trickery *trompe l'oeil* paintings and that any second now you will experience a mental gear shift and see a clear image of the cross and a figure representing Christ on it. No, that is not going to happen. It is a small black painting you see before you. Now, let me tell you what Thomas Merton said in a letter to his friend thanking him for the painting:

> It is a most recollected small painting. It thinks that only one thing is necessary, and this is time, but this one thing is by no means apparent to one who will not take the trouble to look. It is a most religious, devout, and latreutic small painting.[2]

Friends for Life

Thomas Merton had three close friends in his time at Columbia University who influenced various aspects of his life. They influenced him in three key areas: his religious life, art and literature. The friends in question were abstract artist Ad Reinhardt,[3] poet Robert Lax, and poet and writer Edward Rice. The bond of friendship developed from their common interests in matters literary and artistic and lasted throughout their lifetimes. A common thread runs through all of their lives; they were each a seeker after truth and engaged with creative people. They rubbed along very well together and inspired each other by their intellectual debate. They kept in touch at regular intervals after they left university displaying a bond of friendship that was unique in its endurance. It is as though each carried with him something of the other that bonded them, and they needed to touch base occasionally with their shared giftedness in order that each might be fulfilled in his own environment. They were close friends throughout life and influenced one another but each independently forged their own unique careers and lifestyles.

Reinhardt's Influence

It should come as no surprise to anyone that Thomas Merton was an artist. He was after all the son of two artists and the apple did not fall far from the creative tree. It follows that he would be drawn to friendship with the abstract artist Ad Reinhardt, and vice versa. Reinhardt did not see God as the final answer to the search for meaning; for him, art was all that mattered and through good art much truth was revealed. Merton would have agreed with the revelatory power of art; however, he would have said that the ultimate truth is to be found in God. For Merton, art was wonderful, but it was, as he indicated in the response to Reinhardt's gift, something that was at God's service.

I would like to dwell a little longer on Reinhardt's art because it did influence the kind of art that Merton took up in a serious way around the mid 1950s. It was to Reinhardt that he turned for advice and supplies at the time. Like many, I struggle to understand abstract art and I can be quite dismissive of it. Perhaps this dismissal of abstract art is no more than a defensive reaction to the threat of something that we do not understand. We like our art to be accessible – landscapes, portraits and still life. In other words, we like our art to mirror things we are familiar with and are inside our comfort zone. The abstract work of Ad Reinhardt is certainly very challenging for most people to understand.

Reinhardt's Work

Reinhardt was a successful artist and his influence continues to this day. He was regarded as avant-garde, or in that bracket of artist who crossed the boundaries of accepted norms and standards in art. Yet in an almost dictatorial fashion he drew up twelve strict rules that outlined his own views on what he saw as the accepted norms of art, which he wrote in a 1953 essay, 'Twelve Rules for a New Academy'. He searched for what he termed 'pure art' and decried artists who worked to make art accessible and pleasurable for people. Among his rules are the directives that there must be no texture in a painting, no visible brushwork, no sketching or drawing, no forms, no design and no colours. He believed in paring back to the very essence of art, to the essentials. To the casual observer, for Reinhardt the essentials were canvas (any surface), black paint and something with which to apply the paint.

It was his rule of no colour that drew him to black as the one pigment that best expressed pure art. His famous black paintings dominated the last twelve years of his life and they reaffirmed his belief that in art, less is more. He continued to paint black on black until the end of his life, believing that, quite simply, these black paintings were the ultimate art form and all else was meaningless. He claimed he was painting the last paintings – the very end of art.

This description may do little to dispel our misunderstanding of abstract art, and we may well question Reinhardt's appeal to Merton. Equally, we may be puzzled by Merton's positive response to Reinhardt's black paintings, though this may make more sense when we realise that Merton himself was an artist whose artwork could be described as abstract.

Art as Exploration

We know that Merton was drawn to the Eastern religious experience of contemplation and he felt that Buddhism had much to teach the western Christian tradition. As a contemplative, he spent time exploring the depths of solitude. He pressed his superiors to allow him the privilege of a private hermitage on the monastery grounds so that he could be free from distractions and better equipped to explore the mystery of solitude. Like many monastics, he realised that the perfunctory prayer routines, while enriching at many levels, could become monotonous and merely serve as a kind of spiritual dotting the i's and crossing the t's. Merton felt that for most of his life he was struggling with contemplation. He could talk and write about it in detail, but the reality was that he and others only ever reached the foothills of contemplation.

In order to get beyond those foothills, he knew he needed more solitude and the hermit's life offered him that opportunity. The hermitage too offered its own distractions; the toing and froing to the monastery and his writing work took up valuable time. Therefore, he sought other keys to unlocking the mysteries of contemplation and one of those keys was Zen Buddhism. The Buddhist tradition is older by a few centuries than Christianity and both appreciated and shared the contemplative aspects of the spiritual life. Merton found, however, that the monastery and Catholicism were slow to fully embrace all aspects of contemplation. The Zen of the Buddhist tradition can be best described as a clear acceptance that actual meditation is far more important than any form of religious worship and any amount of religious dogma or teaching. I am afraid that the strong yet gentle Zen emphasis will cause the ever-alert guardians of orthodoxy to prick up their ears. In coming to the defence of our Catholic faith they may fault Merton, saying that it was this straying into unorthodoxy that makes him unpalatable and untrustworthy as a spiritual guide. There was no one as orthodox and respectful of Catholic tradition as Thomas Merton. I believe that he was attracted to the Zen in order to learn more from it for himself and even more importantly so that the spiritual thinking and practice of the Catholic Church could learn from it. Merton was an ecumenical thinker who practised a form of shared ecumenical learning that he felt in time could only enrich the indigenous teaching of individual faith traditions.

Merton was deeply impressed by the practice of Zen calligraphy by Buddhist monks. To the uninitiated, this art form seems to be no more that elegant brush strokes resulting in lines, circles, loops and various abstract emblems on a page. Zen calligraphy is much more. It is a process of meditation in which the artist (usually a Buddhist monk) will spend hours in a meditative state staring into the depths of the void before being inspired by those same depths to move his inked brush across the page. Training in such methods and arrival at the painting stage could take years. The resultant design is regarded as the nearest the seeker after truth will come to seeing an earthly imprint or fleeting shadow of the truth that is the divine. In time and with time the viewers of such artistic representations will themselves be aided in their quest for truth by meditating on them. Merton recognised the depth expressed in such images in much the same way as he saw meaning in Reinhardt's small black painting. It is telling too that he saw in that painting the essential quality of time and went so far as to personify the painting itself as capable of thought: 'It thinks that only one thing is necessary and this is time itself.'[4] Merton in the mid to late 1950s was coming into the Zen and learning more from it.

Unlocking the Door

For Merton, the seeker after truth who from both parents had art in his genes, Zen calligraphy was a godsend, literally. He began to paint, draw or compose his own calligraphy as a key to unlocking the door to real and meaningful contemplation. Roger Lipsey, in *Angelic Mistakes: The Art of Thomas Merton*, divides Merton's active engagement with art into three clear periods: his student days at Columbia where he drew cartoon-like illustrations for the undergraduate magazine *The Jester*; his monastic life (1941–56) during which he drew images of the Blessed Virgin, a monk, a crucifixion and other religious representations; and the period from 1960 until his death in 1968, which is of most significance in Merton's art.[5] Throughout all three periods, Merton displayed a sense of freedom and flow in his style of brushwork that reflected some of the subtlety to be seen in the watercolours of his father, Owen Merton.

Merton did not devote a lot of his precious time to his art but slotted it into his already full schedule. Merton and others considered his calligraphic Zen drawings to be good enough for public exhibition. In fact, an exhibition of some thirty of his works travelled to various venues throughout the United States from 1964 to 1967. The fame of the man, already established from his writing, along with the merits of his artwork meant the exhibition was a success. As with his written work, so Merton considered his artwork to be no longer his once it went out into the world. In a sense, this highlights a quintessential aspect of Merton's interest – the process. He saw the actual process of writing itself as a creative force that deepened his spirituality. For Merton, the act of writing reveals as much as the finished piece and this was equally true for his artwork.

Art as Prayer

For Merton the artist, the very process of making art was prayer. His friend Reinhardt would not have put it like that, but he might have accepted that for him art was a substitute for God. Merton and Reinhardt enjoyed lively friendly intellectual banter over issues like the source of creativity and the role, if any, of the divine in art. Merton, the man of faith, was challenged by Reinhardt, the man of no professed faith. Both friends diverged in their beliefs but each respected the other's views and they learned from one another. There is no doubt that Reinhardt shaped Merton's appreciation of abstract art and as a result allowed him to see the value in Zen calligraphy when he came upon it. Merton himself wrote in notes for the exhibition of his own art pieces:

> These abstractions – one might almost call them graffiti rather than calligraphies – are simple signs and ciphers of energy, acts or movements intended to be propitious. Their 'meaning' is not to be sought on the level of convention or of concept.[6]

While one might detect the nervousness of the first-time exhibitor in these words, there is also Merton's own awareness of his own grounding in abstract art and a growing determination to look favourably on the graffiti-like Zen images so that their meaning may come across from within and beneath the surface which is not always in line with the conventional appreciation of art. In other words, he harkens back to his remarks to Reinhardt: 'But this one thing is by no means apparent to one who will not take the trouble to look.'[7]

Photographic Artist

Photography was another art form that Merton took a great interest in and practised in the latter years of his life.

> It was not until Merton discovered that the camera could be an instrument for capturing not shadow but sign, not imitation but image, that he became fascinated by photography.[8]

The camera (usually borrowed) in his hands quickly became an artistic tool and he became proficient in its use. He chose to avoid colour, finding the black and white technique to be far more expressive. When held to his eye the camera ceased to be a mere mechanical instrument but became an X-ray-like extension of his already penetrative eye that saw more than most observers. He brought to photography the same awareness he brought to the maze of abstract forms of art.

On his Asian trip in the weeks before his death he took many fine photographs that now have the added poignancy of being his last works of art. The final photograph taken of Merton shows him lying in his coffin and it seems to capture the sign of serenity and peace that he sought throughout his short life. This photo is the inspiration for the original short poem, 'A Poem for Merton', at the end of this book.

Merton was artistically loaded with ability and talent and was never fazed by anything that interested him. His try-anything attitude led to a deeper awareness of the sub-surface of life. He was drawn to such depths by any means at his disposal – solitude, writing, painting and photography. He went to such places in the hope of finding or getting closer to God.

The Mystery of Never Knowing

If Merton had lived longer, we do not know what advances his art would have taken after his visit to Asia and other subsequent trips. I imagine Merton would say that such speculation is abstraction. Like his friend Reinhardt, he would guide us back to the Zen, the moment of the present in our lives as the daily starting point of our reflection on the mystery of life. Merton saw his art as an instrument of the 'other' in his life. Abstract art does what it says on the tin; it transports us away from the concrete present into another space on the infinitely long journey to and beyond the foothills of contemplation. Reinhardt, Merton and all abstract artists do not seek to explain art but rather suggest you look on it in a propitious light. This involves time and more time in which we the viewers allow ourselves to engage in a two-way silent dialogue with the image before us. More than this, we are encouraged to rest with the subject, be it calligraphic strokes or black squares, and enter into their profound spaciousness so that in time we become aware of our connection with a greater intelligence, a greater power, a loving presence. In this practised self-emptying, we learn to stay quiet and rest in the presence of God. This is what Merton saw as the usefulness and function of art – this latreutic quality of all good art, especially the abstract form which dares to transcend the norm.

Abstract art need not disturb us simply because we do not get an immediate understanding of it. People of faith in God should not be put off by the notion of the abstract. Religious faith itself is an act of trust in the unknown mystery – acknowledgement, acceptance and love of the abstract in our lives. I think this was the path Merton had taken too. He wished for no more than art that would open the portal of mystery and in time lead him to wonder at the hidden garden, that other Eden of William Blake where innocence is reborn and humankind renewed. Merton was a rare fusion of creative leanings – poet, writer, aspiring saint, Zen acolyte, photographer and proponent of the fluid angelic brush stroke.

---

[1] Roger Lipsey, *Angelic Mistakes: The Art of Thomas Merton*, Boston and London: New Seeds, 2006, p. 20.
[2] Letter from Merton to Reinhardt, 23 November 1957, from Joseph Masheck, 'Five Unpublished Letters from Ad Reinhardt to Thomas Merton and Two in Return', *Artforum*, 17, p. 24; quoted in Lipsey, *Angelic Mistakes*, p. 20; 'Latreutic': Of service to God.

[3] Reinhardt graduated from Columbia three months after Merton's arrival, but continued to stay in touch and contribute to the undergraduate magazine *The Jester*.

[4] Letter from Merton to Reinhardt, 23 November 1957, from Masheck, 'Five Unpublished Letters'; quoted in Lipsey, *Angelic Mistakes*, p. 20.

[5] Lipsey, *Angelic Mistakes*, p. 3–6.

[6] Lipsey, *Angelic Mistakes*, p. 60.

[7] Letter from Merton to Reinhardt, 23 November 1957, from Masheck, 'Five Unpublished Letters'; quoted in Lipsey, *Angelic Mistakes*, p. 20.

[8] Christine M. Bochen, William H. Shannon and Patrick F. O'Connell (eds), *The Thomas Merton Encyclopedia*, New York: Orbis Books, 2002, p. 358.

CHAPTER FIVE

Navigating the Work

The best thing that goes on ... is nothing.[1]

Thomas Merton was a compulsive writer. He regarded himself as a poet and writer first, then as a monk and an artist.[2] Gradually he evolved into a monk who is both a writer and an artist. In his twenty-seven years in the monastery Merton the monk-writer published over forty books, averaging almost two a year. One would wonder with the very full schedule of monastic life and a huge volume of incoming and outgoing correspondence where he got the time. His energy and focus were second to none. According to Basil Pennington in his biography of Merton:

> Merton was in the deepest sense of the word a literator. Writing, reading books was part of the fabric of his life. Oftentimes books had more impact on him than personal encounters, or at least they enabled experiences to surface and articulate themselves more clearly and powerfully.[3]

The Book of Life

Wearing his writer's cap, Merton wrote of life as being a book in itself. He had an early take on the contemporary view of writing, which is that everyone has a book in them. For Merton, a fully lived life is the book:

> Perhaps the book of life, in the end, is the book one has lived. If one has lived nothing, one is not in the book of life. I have always wanted to write about everything. That does not mean to write a book that covers

everything – which would be impossible, but a book in which everything can go. A book with a little of everything that creates itself out of nothing. That has its own life. A faithful book. I can no longer look at it as a 'book'.[4]

The Influence of William Blake

Before considering Merton's own works, mention should be made of William Blake (1757–1827), who influenced Merton's outlook from an early age. His father, Owen, admired Blake and introduced his work to Merton. Perhaps, this parental introduction somehow caused Merton to enshrine Blake in his consciousness as someone special because of his father's regard for him. Thomas Merton went on to write a thesis on the art and poetry of William Blake for his master's degree.

Blake was an English poet, artist, philosopher and believer. He was regarded as one of the great anti-heroes of his day, who challenged the religious faith of the time. Though Blake did criticise the Catholic faith, he also spoke of the attractiveness of Catholicism because it was the only religion that taught forgiveness. This is something that would have appealed to Merton, who saw forgiveness for his past as an essential step on his road to conversion and monastic life. William Blake was much maligned and many of his greatest critics were people who felt threatened by his challenge to the religious orthodoxies of the time. Blake questioned much, thought deeply, painted fantastically and sought after a life of contemplation and union with God.

Merton shared some of Blake's qualities: both were highly intellectual; both writers driven by a quest for truth; both conscious of the need for social justice; and both were against war and violence. The parallels between the two men are certainly real and it is clear that Merton was drawn to Blake.

Merton regularly referred to his passion for Blake and made no secret of the fact that his life was influenced by Blake, though less so once he came into his own as a Christian writer, searcher and influencer. In *The Seven Storey*

Mountain, Merton wrote of his experience exploring the work of Blake for his thesis:

> But, oh, what a thing it was to live in contact with the genius and holiness of William Blake that year, that summer, writing the thesis ... He has done his work for me: and he did it very thoroughly. I hope that I will see him in heaven.[5]

Eclectic and Diverse Literary Influences

Apart from his own writing, Merton as master of novices and scholastic master not only shared the wisdom of the Early Church Fathers and classical Spiritual Masters but introduced his students to writers that had inspired him personally. Literary figures including not only the aforementioned Blake, but contemporary figures like James Joyce, Boris Pasternak and poets like Gerard Manley Hopkins and Rainer Maria Rilke. The latter, Rilke, is valued today as having deep religious insights and Merton delivered courses on his themes.[6] Rilke's poem 'Autumn' was a great favourite of Merton:

> The leaves are falling, falling as if from far up,
> as if orchards were dying high in space.
> Each leaf falls as if it were motioning 'no.'
>
> And tonight the heavy earth is falling
> away from all other stars in the loneliness.
>
> We're all falling. This hand here is falling.
> And look at the other one. It's in them all.
>
> And yet there is Someone, whose hands
> infinitely calm, holding up all this falling.[7]

Literary Output

Thomas Merton wrote in a variety of styles and on an array of topics. For our purposes, I have grouped his literary works under the following headings: autobiographical works; monastic topics; biblical works; poetry; the spiritual life; social issues; and Eastern thought. I propose to give a brief insight into each of these. Hopefully, these will act as a guide to the reader who seeks guidance on beginning a voyage of discovery of Merton's work.

Autobiographical Works

The Seven Storey Mountain is Merton's most famous work.[8] It sold over six hundred thousand copies in its first year. It is Merton's 'book of life', 'a book with a little of everything that creates itself out of nothing'.[9] But it is not the entire book and Merton would later come to consider his monastic life and own personal contemplation of God to be the real book of his life. Devotees of Merton's work, however, will always see *The Seven Storey Mountain* as essential reading.

The Sign of Jonas is a follow-on from *The Seven Storey Mountain* and it too sold well. It was written a few years after settling into monastic life in Gethsemani. In it, Merton gives an account of day-to-day life in the monastery and a glimpse into the journey of his spiritual life within the monastic setting. The book's diary-style format makes it easy to dip in and out of whenever the mood suits. In *The Sign of Jonas* we hear echoes of *The Imitation of Christ*, a devotional book by Thomas à Kempis of which Merton was particularly fond in the early years after his reception into the Catholic Church. In recent years, a spiritual book with a similar format called *In Sinu Jesu: When Heart Speaks to Heart: The Journal of a Priest at Prayer* by Dom Mark Kirby of the Silverstream Benedictine Monastery in Meath has become very popular.

A Secular Journal, published in 1959, about twenty years after it was written, is an account of Merton's life and outlook in the immediate years before entering the monastery. It covers the years 1939–41, immediately after his reception into the Catholic Church and entry into the monastery. In an honest and forthright manner, in *A Secular Journal* Merton discerns his vocation as a writer and what form his life's vocation should take within the Church. The book is steeped in the intellectual and literary background of the New York in which Merton lived at that time.

Monastic Topics

After the outstanding success of *The Seven Storey Mountain* the Cistercian authorities realised what a great talent they had in Thomas Merton and enlisted him to write some historical and devotional works on the Cistercian order. This was something that he took to with mixed feelings – more with obedience than enthusiasm.

There was another writer of considerable talent and stature called Fr M. Raymond in the Gethsemani community at that time. Regrettably, a tension arose between Fr Raymond and Fr Louis. It is said it persisted even after Merton's death. James Forest points out the irony that it was Fr Raymond who read aloud *The Seven Storey Mountain*, which was chosen for mealtime readings immediately after Merton's death. Rivalries and petty jealousies are part of everyday life and reflect our human nature in all its glorious and inglorious state. It would be ingenuous to suggest that the cloister is exempt from the full panoply of human behaviours.

The Waters of Siloe takes a general look at the history, background and evolution of the Cistercian order and its various charisms. *The Last of the Fathers* is a short and succinct account of St Bernard of Clairvaux and the encyclical letter of Pope Pius XII, *Doctor Mellifluus*. It is among my favourite of Merton's works. 'What is the monastic life?' Merton asks in the preface and answers:

> It is the life of those who have left the 'world' with its desires and its ambitions in order to devote themselves entirely to seeking God. It is according to St Bernard, a paradise of charity in which it is fully possible for the Christian to live out the baptismal vocation and follow, without half-measures, the Gospel of Christ.[10]

What Are These Wounds?: The Life of a Cistercian Mystic, Saint Lutgarde of Aywières was published in 1948 and is a study of the life of a Cistercian nun of the thirteenth century in Belgium. It is an exposé of her life, her spirituality and her visions. It was dedicated, 'To the Cistercian nuns who are trying to love the Sacred Heart of Jesus in twentieth-century America as He was once loved by their great Patroness St Lutgarde of Aywières.'

The language and style of these devotional monastic writings is dated and hagiographical in tone. One does get a sense that the author was not fully committed or perhaps suited to that particular genre. Merton himself would not rate these works among his best, but they do have their following. Merton had the tendency to move on very quickly from one work to the next; he concerned himself with the work in progress at the time and once finished brought closure on it very quickly.

Many of Merton's thoughts on monastic life are crystallised in *The Monastic Journey*, a volume neatly edited by his personal secretary Br Patrick Hart and published in 1977. The monastic vocation, monastic themes, contemplation and the crisis of faith, the solitary life, along with his ideas for renewal of monasticism are well elaborated in this work.

Biblical Works

It is not surprising to find that Merton had a great feel for and devotion to the sacred scriptures. The daily prayer life of the monastery revolved around the Psalms and scripture readings. Merton's knowledge and love of Latin gave his discussion of the scriptures an added dimension of sacredness. We get a sense of this in a journal entry recorded in 1949, and we see the influence of Gerard Manley Hopkins at play here too:

> Everywhere in Scripture there are doors and windows opened into the same eternity – and the most powerful communication of Scripture is the *insitum verbum* – the engrafted word – the secret, inexpressible seed of contemplation planted in the depths of our soul and awakening it with immediate and inexpressible contact with the Living Word, that we may adore Him in Spirit and Truth. By the reading of Scripture I am so renewed

that all nature seems renewed round me and with me. The sky seems more pure, a cooler blue, the trees a deeper green, light is sharper on the outline of the forest, and the hills and whole world are charged with the glory of God, and I feel fire and music in the earth under my feet.[11]

Monica Furlong in her excellent biography of Merton writes:

One of his constant and never-ending pleasures was the reading of the Scriptures, which resonated in Merton's deep religious imagination, filling his mind with their archetypal images. ... Merton feasted on the scriptures and on the Church Fathers.[12]

His love for and appreciation of the scriptures is evident right through his publications. He published many scripture-related works, notably *Bread in the Wilderness* (1953), *The Living Bread* (1956), *Praying the Psalms* (1956) and *He is Risen* (1975) and a very helpful guide for any reader of the Bible entitled *Opening the Bible* written in 1968, the year he died.

The monastic routine of praying the Psalms made the Psalms themselves a key and favoured part of Thomas Merton's spiritual life. He would have been delighted with the fact that praying the Psalms is no longer the preserve of the priest or religious but is widely used by laypeople for group or personal prayer.

It would be quite wrong to imagine that the prayer life of the Church is divided into two distinct halves, separated by a gap that is rarely bridged, as if the Psalter and the Missal were reserved for clerics and the rosary and other extra liturgical devotions were for the laity.[13]

Merton strove to maintain a respectful middle ground between a scientific and a literal approach to the scriptures. His emphasis was on the fact that the Bible was an inspirational aid to a person's spiritual life. The Bible was not meant to be alien to any believer regardless of their educational background – it was for scholar and non-scholar alike.

Poetry

As a poet, Merton has a keen appreciation of life's poetic pulse in both people and places. He was forever absorbing the poetry of life, as is reflected in a line he wrote describing the view from his room in St Bonaventure University, 'And as the months went on, I began to drink poems out of those hills.'[14]

His visit to Cuba illustrates this strong sense of his imbibing poems from places and people and it is further intensified by the fact that in Cuba he had one of his many deep religious experiences. It was the source of inspiration for his poem 'Song for Our Lady of Cobre', with its striking opening lines that paint the artist-poet's awareness of the subtleties in the movement of people with different skin colour:

> The white girls lift their heads like trees,
> The black girls go
> Reflected like flamingos in the street.
>
> The white girls sing as shrill as water,
> The black girls talk as quiet as clay.[15]

Merton's first published work was a book of poetry. Basil Pennington, while respectful of the poet in Merton and aware of his own inability to do justice to Merton's poetry, writes: 'In the poems we can get in touch with the deeper feelings and intuitions of faith that underlie his actions and his prose writings.'[16]

Yet, Pennington does not hold back when he writes that Merton was at a disadvantage when it came to writing poetry because he was preoccupied with keeping up with the fame of *The Seven Storey Mountain* and hence did not have 'the space and freedom for poetry'.[17] As a result, Pennington says, Merton's later poems are not his best:

He wrote his best verse in his earliest days in the monastery, when he was in some ways most free. His horizons, though, were still quite enclosed, so the poetry tends, with some significant exceptions, towards the pious, lacking the depth of humanity that mark his later writings.[18]

In contrast, Merton's friend Edward Rice is more accepting of his being first and foremost a poet and is clear that the muse never left him:

The spiritual Merton might be dominant, and if so, only by a heroic act of the will, and temporarily, but the creative Merton was never buried. Poems came to him at the most inopportune time, in choir or in meditation and he received permission to put them down.[19]

One can sense a slight undercurrent here – a tug of war between the religious Pennington claiming Merton as spiritual writer and the secular Rice who is pulling for the poetic. I will pull for neither side when it comes to Merton's poetry except to offer my personal appreciation of the poetry of Thomas Merton and to make a claim for him as an outstanding war poet. I make this claim on the strength of his most quoted poem, 'For My Brother: Reported Missing in Action, 1943', which he wrote in memory of his brother John Paul, who died after his aircraft was shot down in World War II. It puts Merton high in the ranks of war poets especially those who wrote in World War I. Merton writes:

Where in what desolate and smokey country,
Lies your poor body, lost and dead?
And in what landscape of disaster
Has your unhappy spirit lost its road?[20]

It has echoes of John McCrae's World War I poem 'In Flanders Fields' (1915):

We are the Dead. Short days ago
We lived, felt dawn, saw sunset glow,
Loved and were loved, and now we lie,
In Flanders fields.

Merton's poem is also redolent of Laurence Binyon's 'For the Fallen' (1914):

They shall not grow old, as we that are left grow old.

The loss of his only sibling marked the end of the family unit that began in Prades in 1915. Naturally, it affected him greatly and the poet drank a poem from the bitter cup of loss. We can only speculate as to how aware Merton was of the war poets or whether he had read WB Yeats's poem 'An Irish Airman Foresees His Death' (1919). Gerard Manley Hopkins's near-metaphysical imagery and language appealed to Merton's own quest for inner truth. His poem for his brother is evocative too of Hopkins's great lament poem 'The Wreck of the Deutschland', which was written in memory of five Franciscan nuns who were among the drowning victims. Merton's lament for his brother matches Hopkins's faith-charged lines:

—Hither then, last or first,
To hero of Calvary, Christ's feet—
Never ask if meaning it, wanting it, warned of it— men go.[21]

Mark Van Doren, a lifelong literary friend, comments:

For Merton there is another world beyond this one where his brother died, and where he himself writes poetry. But the poetry is a way to that world. Indeed, given his endowment, it may well be *the* way, so that mystic and poet, seer and singer, in this case are one.[22]

One other favourite of mine is a Merton poem entitled 'A Psalm', which captures his love of scripture and the Psalms that were the bread and butter of his daily monastic prayer:

When psalms surprise me with their music
And antiphons turn to rum
The Spirit sings: the bottom drops out of my soul

And from the center of my cellar, Love, louder than the
thunder
Opens a heaven of naked air.[23]

The poet Merton drank poetry from many sources, but as a poet of religious intent one senses he breathed the naked air of heaven as his inspiration.

The Spiritual Life

Merton was not unlike St John Henry Newman in returning to the early fathers as a source of inspiration. He loved the wisdom he found in the desert fathers, Cassian, Clement of Alexandria, St John Chrysostom, St Jerome, Tertullian and others. He tried to absorb all he could from their writing on and practice of solitude and time apart from the world. Daniel Berrigan wrote, 'Merton does not so much introduce the Fathers of the desert; he stands in their midst, one of them.'[24]

We see the fruit of Merton's endeavours in works like *The Wisdom of the Desert, Ways of the Christian Mystics, An Introduction to Christian Mysticism, Cassian and the Fathers.* Thomas Merton also had an affinity with the English, Spanish and Russian mystics.

Since his reception into the Catholic Church, Merton had been a keen disciple of John of the Cross, the sixteenth-century Carmelite mystic, poet and theologian who became a doctor of the Church. Merton's *The Ascent to the Truth* portrays John of the Cross's journey to the highest summit of truth, 'The truth man needs ... God himself', reached in the depths of contemplation. The pathway to this intimate union is through detachment and unworldliness, a reaching into the depths to gain great heights.

Merton is most appreciated for his work describing various aspects of the spiritual life. Those drawn to a deepening of spiritualty feel that Merton excelled in writing about the experience of the spiritual life. His books in this area include *Thoughts in Solitude, No Man is an Island, The New Man, Life and Holiness, Seeds of Contemplation, New Seeds of Contemplation, Contemplation in a World of Action, Spiritual Direction and Meditation* and *What is Contemplation?*

The aforementioned works take us to the heart of what I and others regard as Merton's greatest contribution to the spiritual quest of the modern person. Merton encouraged everyone, not just clergy and religious, to be contemplatives. I have no doubt following on the thrust of the Second Vatican Council, his encouragement was one of the reasons for the growth in the number of laypeople doing retreats and taking the spiritual life seriously in an informed way. He takes a gentle, gradual and sensible approach:

> If we really want prayer, we'll have to give it time. We must slow down to a human tempo and we'll begin to have time to listen. And as soon as we listen to what's going on, things will begin to take shape by themselves.[25]

The direct, down-to-earth, pull-no-punches teacher leaves us under no illusions about the difficulty of the journey:

> If you have never had any distractions you don't know how to pray. For the secret of prayer is a hunger for God and for the vision of God, a hunger that lies far deeper than the level of language or affection. And a man whose memory and imagination are persecuting him with a crowd of useless or even evil thoughts and images may sometimes be forced to pray far better, in the depths of his murdered heart, than one whose mind is swimming with clear concepts and brilliant purposes and easy acts of love.[26]

He points out the practical benefits and graces of effective prayer:

If well made, my meditation will bear fruit in an increase of fortitude in patience. My patience will help me endure trials in such a way that my soul will be purified of many imperfections and obstacles to grace. I will learn to know better the source of anger in my life. I will then grow in charity.[27]

He writes about the attractive fruits of the contemplative life in a writing style reminiscent of John Henry Newman:

The contemplative life has nothing to tell you except to reassure you and say that if you dare to penetrate your own silence and dare to advance without fear into the solitude of your own heart and risk the sharing of that solitude with the lonely other who seeks God through you and with you, then you will truly recover the life and the capacity to understand what is beyond words and beyond explanations because it is too close to be explained: it is the intimate union in the depths of your heart, of God's spirit and your own innermost self, so that you and He are in truth One Spirit.[28]

We can only marvel at the amount of classic spiritual works Fr Louis produced in his few decades in the monastery. He squeezed his writing into a few hours each day as much as he could manage in the full schedule of prayer and other activities in the monastery. He worked on a simple electric typewriter and only in later years with the assistance of a personal secretary, Br Patrick Hart. Again, we can only imagine what he would have produced with the aid of modern conveniences.

Social Issues

There were three distinct phases in the life of Thomas Merton: his being in the world; his being apart from the world; and then his bridging the monastic world and the world outside the monastery. Merton's experience of being 'in the world' was not an entirely happy one and is well documented in *The Seven Storey Mountain*. His time of withdrawal from the world in the monastery helped him regain perspective and having set his own inner house in order, he became more outward-looking and began to consider and comment on the many social issues of his day.

Much of his thinking on social issues is found in works like *Raids on the Unspeakable*, *The New Man* and *Seeds of Destruction*.

The title of one of the best works of his last decade, *Conjectures of a Guilty Bystander*, speaks of his growing sense of regret at not being more immersed in some of the concerns of the time. Issues of the day such as racism, war and peace, civil rights and social unrest became very concerning for him. It is a book worth reflecting on from a modern perspective as it has much to teach us. In the same book he presents an interesting critique of the business world that might apply today:

> Businesses are, in reality, quasi-religious sects. When you go to work in one you embrace a *new faith*. And if they are really big businesses, your progress from faith to a kind of mystique. Belief in the product, preaching the product, in the end the product becomes the focus of a transcendental experience. Through the 'product' one communes with the vast forces of life, nature and history that are expressed in business. Why not face it? Advertising treats all products with the reverence and the seriousness due to sacraments.[29]

He speaks of clearing the clutter of the modern world:

> The greatest need of our time is to clean out the enormous mass of mental and emotional rubbish that clutters our minds and makes all political and social life a mass illness.[30]

He goes on to speak of what he calls the 'technological imperative':

It does us no good to make fantastic progress if we do not know how to live with it, if we cannot make good use of it, and if, in fact, our technology becomes nothing more than an expensive and complicated way of cultural disintegration. It is bad form to say such things, to recognize such possibilities. But they are possibilities, and they are not often intelligently taken into account. People get emotional about them from time to time, and then try to sweep them aside into forgetfulness. The fact remains that we have created for ourselves a culture which is not yet livable for mankind as a whole.[31]

Peace and racism were two social issue of particular concern for Merton. He has been described as the 'conscience of the peace movement in the 1960s' and the Thomas Merton Center for Peace and Justice was formed in the early 1970s to promote his ideas on the issue.[32] In 1963, he wrote *Letters to a White Liberal*, which became the basis of *Seeds of Destruction*, at the height of racial tensions in the United Stated. His poem in memory of Martin Luther King Jr is worth recalling in this context:

April 4th 1968
For Martin Luther King

On a rainy night
On a rainy night in April
When everybody ran
Said the minister

On a balcony
Of a hotel in Tennessee
'We came at once
Upstairs'

On a night
On a rainy night in April
When the shot was fired
Said the minister

'We came at once upstairs
And found him lying

After the tornado
On the balcony
We came at once upstairs'

On a rainy night
He was our hope
And we found a tornado
Said the minister.

And a well-dressed white man
Said the minister.
Dropped the telescopic storm

And he ran
(The well-dressed minister of death) He ran
He ran away

And on the balcony
Said the minister
We found
Everybody dying.[33]

Eastern Thought

From his early days, Thomas Merton cast his sights towards faraway green hills in the expectation of hues that were fresher and greener. From infancy, he was accustomed to frequent interchange with the cultures of a number of countries and continents. It is perhaps not surprising that his literary and religious interests knew no boundaries either.

Having studied the early desert fathers and the medieval mystics, somewhat like Alexander the Great having no more immediate worlds to conquer, he set his sights on broadening his vista with the wisdom of the East. Much of his thought is brought together in works like *The Asian Journal, Mystics and Zen Masters, Zen and the Birds of Appetite, Thoughts on the East.* Merton was as much at home with the masters of the Zen, Buddhist, Hindu, Islamic and Tao traditions as he was with Christianity. In the estimation of Michael W. Higgins, 'He didn't discover the East: the East discovered him.'[34]

Whether it was the Dalai Lama or DT Suzuki, Merton could hold his own and add to the exchange of views with his creative, artistic, literary and poetic mind. This same disposition enabled him to see links between eastern wisdom and Christianity. East and West have much to learn from one another's traditions. It was his view that:

> we cannot really understand Chinese Zen if we do not grasp the implicit Buddhist metaphysic which it so to speak acts out. But the Buddhist metaphysic itself is hardly doctrinal in our elaborate philosophical and theological sense: Buddhist philosophy is an interpretation of ordinary human experience, but an interpretation which is not revealed by God nor discovered in the access of inspiration nor seen in a mystical light. Basically, Buddhist metaphysics is a very simple and natural elaboration of the implications of God's own experience of enlightenment. Buddhism does not seek primarily to understand or to 'believe in' the enlightenment of Buddha as the solution to all human problems, but seeks an existential and empirical participation in that enlightenment experience.[35]

Thomas Merton was on the cusp of enlightening the Christian world through what he was exploring in Asian traditions. His wisdom and scholarship were capable of piecing together the many fragmented approaches of various faith traditions into a unified synthesis. It was not to be, however, because his life on earth was brought to an abrupt end. Merton's legacy is his collection of writing, which can be analysed in order to seek the unity between all religious believers he felt was close at hand.

It must be stressed, however, that Merton was not so much concerned with religious unity as he was with each religious tradition respecting each other's faith tradition. Edward Rice puts it thus:

> He did not try to 'baptize' Buddhism as the average Christian might. He was not interested in picking odds

and ends from the East and amalgamating them into Christianity. Buddhism has its own very valid and true existence, and he was trying to shed the restrictions of the Western mind in reaching out for it. He went through tremendous growing pains in each step of his life and each meant a major upheaval. His study of the East was such an experience.[36]

Merton's sudden death put an end to his Eastern journey (physical, emotional and spiritual) and began the wave of speculation as to his future within or outside the cloister. A forest of 'what ifs' grew, speculating on whether he would have embraced Buddhism and stayed in the East or returned to Gethsemani for short intervals, coming and going as a nomadic monk. It is entertaining to speculate, but Merton being Merton would have discerned and done his own thing that may well have been totally opposite to the indicators we like to think showed us where his life might have been going.

Regardless of the 'what ifs', I feel his life would have been exciting and beneficial to a church whose world view was radically changing at the time of his death. I return to his letter to Pope John XXIII in which he wrote:

> It seems to me that, as a contemplative, I do not need to lock myself into solitude and lose all contact with the rest of the world; rather this poor world has a right to my solitude.[37]

Yes, we are blessed to have the legacy of Merton's writings and if he had lived longer, I think we would have been further blessed to share that unlocked solitude.

Reaction

Merton was sensitive to the reaction of others both within the Church and outside it. From an early stage within the order he came up against the obstacle of censorship and this was a source of considerable anger and frustration to Merton. His interaction with people like Evelyn Waugh was a considerable help to him in establishing his own unique style and he was open to constructive criticism.

Certainly, he had his supporters and detractors and many of the detractors were within the Church. It is interesting to note that three popes – John XXIII, Paul VI and Pope Francis – appreciated Merton. Pope John XXIII honoured him in his lifetime with the personal gift of a papal stole and engaged in correspondence with him. Pope Paul VI gifted him with a crucifix. Pope Francis in a 2015 address to the American Congress spoke of Thomas Merton as a visionary American who 'remains a source of spiritual inspiration and a guide for many people'.[38]

One would like to think that the support of such notable popes might go some small way to softening the cough of Merton's most ardent detractors. Either way, the fact remains that Thomas Merton is a giant who has survived Lilliputian put-downs from critics within and outside the Church. Thankfully, his rich legacy continues to edify, entertain and instruct us to this day.

---

[1] M. Basil Pennington, *Thomas Merton, Brother Monk: The Quest for True Freedom*, San Francisco: Harper and Row, 1987, p. 1.

[2] Ibid., p. 27.

[3] Ibid., p. 58.

[4] Journal entry, 17 July 1956 in Patrick Hart and Jonathan Montaldo (eds), *The Intimate Merton: His Life from His Journals*, Oxford: Lion Publishing, 2000, p. 113.

[5] *The Seven Storey Mountain*, pp. 189–90.

[6] *God Speaks to Each of Us: The Poetry and Letters of Rainer Maria Rilke*, lecture series narrated by Thomas Merton, Gethsemani Classroom Series: Now You Know Media, 2013.

[7] Rainer Maria Rilke, 'Autumn', *Poems of Rainer Maria Rilke*, Jessie Lamont (trans.), Auckland: The Floating Press, 2012.

[8] The English edition was entitled *Elected Silence*, referencing the Gerard Manley Hopkins poem, 'The Habit of Perfection' (1918), which begins:
Elected Silence, sing to me
And beat upon my whorled ear,
Pipe me to pastures still and be
The music that I care to hear.

[9] Journal entry, 17 July 1956 in Hart and Montaldo (eds), *The Intimate Merton*, p. 113.

¹⁰ *The Last of the Fathers: Saint Bernard of Clairvaux and the Encyclical Letter, Doctor Mellifluus*, p. 13.
¹¹ Journal entry, 8 August 1949, *Entering the Silence:Volume II, 1941–1952*, p. 349–50.
¹² Monica Furlong, *Merton: A Biography*, San Francisco: Harper and Row, 1980, p. 188.
¹³ *Praying The Psalms*, p. 15.
¹⁴ *The Seven Storey Mountain*, p. 333.
¹⁵ *The Collected Poems of Thomas Merton*, New York: New Directions, 1977, p. 29.
¹⁶ Pennington, *Thomas Merton, Brother Monk*, p. 199.
¹⁷ Ibid., p. 37.
¹⁸ Ibid., p. 37.
¹⁹ Edward Rice, *The Man in the Sycamore Tree: The Good Times and Hard Life of Thomas Merton*, New York: Image Books, 1972, pp. 82–3.
²⁰ *The Collected Poems of Thomas Merton*, p. 35. Full poem included in chapter eight of this publication.
²¹ Gerard Manley Hopkins, 'The Wreck of the Deutschland', *The Works of Gerard Manley Hopkins*, London: Wordsworth Editions, 1994, p. 14.
²² Mark Van Doren, Introduction, *Selected Poems of Thomas Merton*, New York: New Directions, 1967.
²³ *The Collected Poems of Thomas Merton*, p. 220.
²⁴ Back cover of *The Wisdom of the Desert*, New York: New Directions, 1970.
²⁵ Basil Pennington, *Centering Prayer: Renewing an Ancient Christian Prayer Form*, New York: Doubleday, 1980, p. 56.
²⁶ *New Seeds of Contemplation*, p. 221.
²⁷ *Spiritual Direction and Meditation*, p. 59.
²⁸ *The Monastic Journey*, Patrick Hart (ed.), New York: New Directions, 1978, p. 173.
²⁹ *Conjectures of a Guilty Bystander*, p. 84.
³⁰ *Conjectures of a Guilty Bystander*; quoted in Robert Inchausti, *Thomas Merton's American Prophesy*, Albany: State University of New York Press, 1998, p. 149.
³¹ *Conjectures of a Guilty Bystander*; quoted in Robert Inchausti (ed.), *The Pocket Thomas Merton*, Boston: New Seeds, 2005, p. 51.
³² Inchausti, *Thomas Merton's American Prophesy*, p. 93.
³³ *The Collected Poems of Thomas Merton*, p. 1005.
³⁴ Michael W. Higgins, *Thomas Merton: Faithful Visionary*, Minnesota: Liturgical Press, 2014, p. 104.
³⁵ *Zen and the Birds of Appetite*, p. 77.
³⁶ Edward Rice, *The Man in the Sycamore Tree*, pp. 130–1.
³⁷ Letter from Thomas Merton to Pope John XXIII, 10 November 1958; quoted in Lawrence Cunningham, *Thomas Merton and the Monastic Vision*, Cambridge: William B. Eerdmans Publishing Company, 1999, p. 64.
³⁸ Pope Francis, Address of the Holy Father to the Joint Session of the United States Congress, Washington, DC, 24 September 2015, http://www.vatican.va/content/francesco/en/speeches/2015/september/documents/papa-francesco_20150924_usa-us-congress.html

CHAPTER SIX

Social Issues: Then and Now

Your dark eyes will never
Need to understand
Our sadness[1]

Thomas Merton's main social concerns were in the area of peace and anti-racism. His thinking on both was honest, forthright and uncompromising. He was regarded as a leading exponent of human rights for Black America as well as a leading dove of peace. Both issues unsettled him and made him unpopular with his own religious order, the Catholic Church and many people in America. Some would have preferred Merton to remain silent on these issues and observe the detached monkish position of simply praying about them from the distance of his hermit's life. He wrote, 'It seems illusory if I do not in some way identify myself with the cause of people who are denied their rights and forced, for the most part, to live in abject misery.'[2]

It would disappoint Merton, though not surprise him, that issues of both peace and racism are still contentious fifty-two years after his death. Merton sensed that the pathway to any real change in people's outlook required a conversion or radical awakening on an individual and personal basis. It was an awakening he experienced in his own life.

Fourth and Walnut

Merton had struggled with his re-engagement with the secular world. He struggled until he had what is now referred to as his 'Fourth and Walnut' moment. On 18 March 1958 he was visiting Louisville and he had an experience on the street corner of Fourth and Walnut that reconciled him to the beauty and grace of the world he had left behind. On entering the monastery, he felt the world was a place almost irredeemable where people were destined for unhappiness. All that changed on Fourth and Walnut as he observed the passers-by:

> In Louisville, at the corner of Fourth and Walnut, in the center of the shopping district, I was suddenly overwhelmed with the realization that I loved all these people, that they were mine and I theirs, that we could not be alien to one another even though we were total strangers. It was like waking from a dream of separateness, of spurious self-isolation in a special world.
>
> This sense of liberation from an illusory difference was such a relief and such a joy to me that I almost laughed out loud ... I have the immense joy of being man, a member of a race in which God Himself became incarnate. As if the sorrows and stupidities of the human condition could overwhelm me, now that I realize what we all are. And if only everybody could realize this! But it cannot be explained. There is no way of telling people that they are all walking around shining like the sun.
>
> Then it was as if I suddenly saw the secret beauty of their hearts, the depths of their hearts where neither sin nor desire nor self-knowledge can reach, the core of their reality, the person that each one is in God's eyes. If only they could all see themselves as they really are. If only we could see each other that way all the time. There would be no more war, no more hatred, no more greed ... But this cannot be seen, only believed and 'understood' by a peculiar gift.[3]

This 'peculiar gift' reminds me of a description in an Edna O'Brien short story of an old woman speaking of that impenetrable space in one's mind called the God Particle:

That's what an old woman in the village used to call it, that last cranny where you say your prayers and confide in yourself the truth of what you feel about everything and everyone.[4]

Merton's experience seems to have come from that space – the God Particle – and it has been described, rightly, as mystical. It was a mystical experience that is memorialised in a plaque on the spot in downtown Louisville. The experience further moved Merton to realise his human identity as being one with all creeds and races in the United States and worldwide. He wrote about it in a letter to James Baldwin:

> I am therefore not completely human until I have found myself in my African and Asian and Indonesian brother because he has the part of humanity which I lack.[5]

Merton's words laid the foundation for his anti-racist stance and its prescience is seen in its relevance to the race situation today. It all grew from that mystical moment on Fourth and Walnut. It is the kind of moment people wish for in their lives, or in Merton's words, 'If only we could see each other that way all the time.'[6]

Whether he was dealing with issues of peace or racial injustice, Merton was unashamedly Christian in his approach. The teaching of Christ was to the fore at all times in his writings and pronouncements. It was perhaps his near-dogged adherence to gospel values and truth that made Church authorities uncomfortable and hence annoyed at what they perceived as his impertinent insistence on Christ's teaching. He unfailingly put forward the view that war was wrong and that the Christian must be opposed to it at all times:

> What are we to do? The duty of the Christian in this crisis is to strive with all his power and intelligence, with his faith, hope in Christ, and love for God and humanity, to do the one task which God has imposed

upon us in the world today. That task is to work for the total abolition of war.[7]

For Merton, a Catholic has no choice in the matter but to be opposed to war and racial inequality. It is a given for a faith that was founded on Jesus' two great commandments: to love God with all your heart, all your soul and with all your mind; and to love your neighbour as yourself (Mk 12:28–34). The notion of slavery is alien to such a faith and to think that racism in any form was acceptable would be anathema to this faith.

Pacem in Terris

The protest movement of the 1960s engaged Merton greatly. He wrote about the threat of nuclear war and the government's need to promote militarism at all costs as a means to achieving peace. Merton was a pacifist and a pacifist who loved all of humanity regardless of creed or colour. His belief in pacifism might be regarded as naive in not accounting for the need for countries to protect against possible aggressors. After all, America prided itself on being the nation that came to the aid of Europe during World War II. Merton appreciated the dichotomy of the just war and the desire for peace. He had a simple starting point as he showed in a passing phrase in *The Sign of Jonas*, 'Wars are evil but the people involved in them are good.'

Monica Furlong points out that during the 1960s, Merton was often enduring severe ill health which debilitated him but yet did not seem to lessen his literary output.[8] One could perhaps assume that ill health added extra stridency to his writings on war and peace. Likewise, we cannot overlook the fact that the shadows of two world wars fell on Merton during his lifetime. Losing his only brother, John Paul, in World War II surely reinforced his pacifist stance. John Paul had recently converted to Catholicism and Merton laments him in that Christo-centric approach he took to his stance on war and racism. His was a Christ who sacrificed himself for humanity and in John Paul's death Merton saw the Cross of Christ:

Your cross and mine shall tell men still
Christ died on each, for both of us.
For in the wreckage of your April Christ lies slain,
And Christ weeps in the ruins of my spring:[9]

Merton carried the weight of the loss of his brother and it became a catalyst for his campaign for peace. Ironically, advocating peace brought little peace into his life. He was appalled at the manner in which the Christian world accepted the nuclear bomb as something awful but necessary for the saving of humankind. There was in society a reluctance to look deeper into the causes of war and the general optics in which the Church tolerated the nuclear bomb. For Merton, it was a case of God's gift of humanity betraying humanity. He wrote, 'We must try to remember that the enemy is as human as we are, and not an animal or a devil.'[10]

Merton's views on war and peace did not sit well with American political society and outlook. His own order felt he was overstepping the mark by entering what was considered the political arena. The censors of the order forbade him to write any further on the topic of peace. In the same year (1963), Pope John XXIII's encyclical *Pacem In Terris* (*Peace on Earth*) appeared and took Merton's thinking even further. As Monica Furlong explains, *Pacem In Terris*:

> was in itself a piece of writing that went far beyond the usual empty utterances of pontiffs and archbishops, and which tried, as Merton was trying, to reach the roots of the terrible problem that was tearing the world apart. But Merton was told that he did not know enough about the problems he was writing about and that the task should be left to others who did.[11]

The irony was not lost on Merton, but one assumes his respect for John XXIII and the encyclical's strong sentiments would have pleased him. Merton continued to write and advocate for peace and his involvement with Fr Dan Berrigan and others continued in the years up to his death. It is not my intention to outline the history of Merton's involvement with the peace movement, but simply to highlight the core principle of Christian teaching on which he based his views about war and peace. It was as fundamental as the fifth commandment (Thou shalt not kill) and grounded in the greatest commandment, to love God and love your neighbour. The same Christian principle was the foundation for his anti-racist stance.

Mutually Complete One Another

One need search no further for a summation of Merton's views on race than the line, 'They are brothers in the fullest sense of the word.'[12] Were he writing today he would be sensitive to the inclusivity of language and put it thus, 'They are brothers and *sisters* in the fullest sense of the word.' Likewise, Merton used the word 'negro', which was used up to the late 1960s when it was replaced by the word 'Black'.

As in the case of the Peace Movement, Merton was motivated by the gospel values of equality and love when speaking of the issue of race. He went so far to say that Catholicism was an ideal vehicle for understanding and solving racial discrimination.

> A genuinely Catholic approach to the Negro would assume not only that the white and the Negro are essentially equal indignity (and this, I think we do generally assume) but also that they are brothers in the fullest sense of the word. This means to say a genuinely Catholic attitude in matters of race is one which concretely accepts and fully recognizes the fact that different races and cultures are correlative. They mutually complete one another. The white man needs the Negro, and needs to know that he needs him. White calls for black just as black calls for white. Our significance as white men is to be seen entirely in the fact that all men are not white. Until this fact is grasped, we will never realize our true place in the world, and we will never achieve what we are meant to achieve in it.[13]

This astounding statement by Merton sets the unflinching tone of his approach to racism. It is as valid today as it was back then. For some it is too idealistic whereas Merton and others would rightly hold that racism will always prevail unless everyone has a personal conversion or Fourth and Walnut moment so that in his words:

> if only we could see each other that way all the time. There would be no more war, no more hatred, no more greed ... But this cannot be seen, only believed and 'understood' by a peculiar gift.[14]

The gift is a change of heart that must happen in the God space of every human being.

The Zeal of the Convert

Merton's love of place was always to the fore in his life and writers have remarked on his youthful jaunts into Harlem in search of good jazz. Similarly, as a young lecturer in St Bonaventure University he worked for a while with Baroness Catherine de Hueck Doherty (well known for her book *Poustinia*), who ran a centre for disadvantaged people in Harlem called Friendship House. Merton thought he might have found the answer to his search for meaning and fulfilment in his work in Harlem; but his answer lay in his conversion to Catholicism and entry into the monastic life.

His views on racism and peace were radical in the sense that they were founded on the basic tenets of Catholicism. Being a convert, he was less burdened with the compromises that the cradle Catholic tends to make on issues of social justice. Merton made no compromises in his thinking and as a result he was both saddened and pessimistic about the slow progress in eliminating racism in not only America but throughout the world.

'Social Issues: Then and Now' is the title of this chapter. I have focused on the then of Merton's time and his views. There is hardly any need to point out the parallels between then and now – they are unmissable. The now is being written daily with the Black Lives Matter protests. Half a century after his death, Merton's words resonate prophetically and with fresh significance.

---

[1] 'Picture of a Black Child with a White Doll', *The Collected Poems of Thomas Merton*, New York: New Directions, 1977, p. 626.

[2] *Seeds of Destruction*.

[3] *Conjectures of a Guilty Bystander*, pp. 153–4.

[4] Edna O'Brien, 'Plunder', *Saints and Sinners*, London: Faber and Faber, 2012, p. 82.

[5] Merton to Baldwin, 1964; quoted in Robert Inchausti (ed.), *Echoing Silence: Thomas Merton on the Vocation of Writing*, Boston: New Seeds, 2007, p. 128.

[6] *Conjectures of a Guilty Bystander*, p. 142.

[7] Uncensored addition to *New Seeds of Contemplation*.

[8] Monica Furlong, *Merton: A Biography*, San Francisco: Harper and Row, 1980, p. 272.

[9] 'For My Brother: Reported Missing in Action, 1943', *The Collected Poems of Thomas Merton*, New York: New Directions, 1977, p. 35.

[10] Thomas Merton (ed.), *Breakthrough to Peace: Twelve Views on the Threat of Thermonuclear Extermination*, New York: New Directions, 1962.

[11] Furlong, *Merton: A Biography*, pp. 257–8.

[12] Thomas Merton, *Passion for Peace: Reflections on War and Nonviolence, 1961–1968*, William H. Shannon (ed.), New York: Crossroad, 1997, p. 183.

[13] Ibid.

[14] *Conjectures of a Guilty Bystander*, p. 154.

CHAPTER SEVEN

Living with Merton

It is not as an author that I would speak to you, not as a storyteller, not as a philosopher, not as a friend only: I seek to speak to you in some way as your own self.[1]

Thomas Merton died in 1968 at the age of fifty-three. For one so young he had lived through much turmoil, including two world wars. As an infant, he was oblivious to the first and the cocoon of the monastery cut him off from much of the reality of World War II. Yet, his first published work had a great impact on a world recovering from war. How is it that a man who was a pacifist at heart and sat out (knelt out if you like) the war had such influence on the world? Also, I might add this other question: has this man any relevance to the world as we know it today?

Those who knew Merton in life knew a man of great good humour, a lover of jazz and a good time, but at the same time a man who exuded a sense of a deep inner strength. How blessed they were to have known him and to be able to hear him speak aloud, or even in the silent signing language of the monastery. Thankfully, some tapes of Merton's lectures to his novices remain and they are worth listening to for both their content and the pleasant warm timbre of his voice. I noticed on listening to his lectures that like many he had a speech mannerism. Every now and then he would punctuate his speech in a quizzical tone with the word 'see'. There I think lies the key to understanding Merton. That speech mannerism was gently provocative and persistently spoken with an eager hope that the listeners would be able to understand what he was imparting to them. I think it also answers my two questions about his past influence and his relevance today: Merton was a 'seer'. I use the word 'seer' not in any wizardly sense but rather in the sense of his being one who took time to see into the depths of his own being and in the sense that his thinking and written work were visionary and continue to remain so to this day.

Enduring Constant

Merton lived in a world that was electrified by change and which presented novel and exciting challenges to the thinkers of his day. It was the era of the beatnik and hippy, the dropout, the engaged civil rights movement, the Vietnam War protests, the space race, the Cold War, nuclear power, *Pacem in Terris* and the advent of the Second Vatican Council. This eclectic mix of issues and events heightened tensions and inspired action and reaction in all walks of life.

Fifty-two years after Merton's death the world has changed dramatically. Are we deluding ourselves by thinking that a man who lived most of his days in an isolated cell in a Trappist monastery in rural Kentucky is still relevant to our world today? We can only look to Merton's engagement with the world of his time to find an answer to that question.

Merton's influence on the world during his lifetime began and has lasted from the publication of *The Seven Storey Mountain* to this day. In actual living time it was a mere twenty years, but it was a highly productive twenty years. His influence arose first and foremost from his personal witness to his faith.

Merton's life in those years had a dual aspect to it – the public and the private life. The naysayers suggest that in his interaction with the world outside the monastery Merton somehow betrayed himself and his calling to the monastic life. They would suggest that the published Merton overtook the private life and that from 1948 onwards he lived only a public life.

They overlook that complementary duality of private and public. His harshest critics wanted Merton to remain the stereotypical monk with the quill in his hand as he stooped over the page scratching out his thoughts. They would have preferred it thus; that he simply stayed put.

It was his spirituality and love of God and Mary that grounded him at all times and his life was one constant revolution around the axle of prayer and devotional exercises. It is this grounding that made his influence felt in the world of his day and which has made his message endure. It is a message that reflects and is faithful to the eternal message of Jesus Christ. The motto of the Carthusians, whom Thomas Merton seriously considered joining, is *Stat crux dum volvitur orbis*, 'The Cross is steady while the world is turning.' The world changes, but the Cross and the eternal truths of the mystery of Christianity remain a constant – Christ yesterday, today and tomorrow – always the same. Merton stood by the steadying influence of that Cross.

For many people today, the inspirational writings of Thomas Merton are an enduring constant. They are a steadying support in their spiritual lives as they seek deeper insights into prayer and an entry into the world of contemplation on that path of life where truth beckons and inner-peace smiles.

Search for Meaning

Merton sought after the true meaning of life and he came to realise very early on in his search that God represented the true meaning. In a sense the simplicity of this truth may take the shine off the search for some people. Surely, they feel, it requires far more searching before arrival at an answer. Merton spent his life searching not for meaning (he had already found it in his faith) but rather he searched for new meanings and new approaches to focus one's attention on and find ways to freshly focus on God – the meaning of life.

The appeal of Merton's work to our modern world is that there is a common thread throughout. Starting with *The Seven Storey Mountain*, and throughout his vast literary output, he relates in a down-to-earth manner to the spiritual and existential struggles of the modern woman and man.

I believe that modern-day readers will be assisted to discern the will of God for them on an individual basis. Merton speaks to the very ordinariness of all our lives. It is said often that Merton's genius lies in the 'extraordinary ordinariness' of the way he relates to us.

Merton was never more at peace than when he prayed and it was in the solitude of the hermitage that he found most peace. Yet life was never plain sailing for him and he struggled for decades to find that middle ground between interaction with the outside world and the quietude of the monastic life.

He had struggled as a young man with the meaninglessness of the hedonistic life of his youthful college days. In later years while in the monastery he struggled with the demands of the outside world with its pressing needs caused by mounting industrialisation and the materialism of American society.

He struggled to send a message from behind the monastery walls to a world where the growth of individualism, indifferentism, utilitarianism and relativism had become the jungle of diverse attraction in which the message of Christ was in danger of going unheard and unnoticed.

He struggled too with his vocation to the quiet life of the monastery and the existential loneliness of the enclosed monk. The spirit was at all times willing but he realised too the weakness of flesh which ached at times like all humanity for earthly companionship. The modern reader will find comfort in the fact that Merton struggled and at times faltered in his commitment to his chosen life.

We can admire the inner loyalty of Merton, a high achiever who doggedly focused on and dedicated himself to what he put his mind to – mediocrity was never an option for him. He took on an enormous workload and divided his day between various tasks and not surprisingly he did not spare himself in his application to the spiritual life.

Gradually the truth of what his friend Robert Lax had said to him that day on Sixth Avenue in spring of 1939 began to dawn on him, that anyone's true vocation was to strive to the high ideal of being a saint. In the words of the French novelist and convert to the faith, Léon Bloy, 'The only tragedy in life is not to be a saint.'[2] Merton in a lifetime of effort and dedication as a writer and monk certainly made a good stab at it.

A Prophetic Voice

Merton was of his time and in a sense, he was also ahead of his time. His interest and passion for the social issues of the day are perhaps best expressed in *The Seeds of Destruction* and *Conjectures of a Guilty Bystander*. We see from the latter title that in some ways he almost regretted his distance from the affairs of the world during the second phase of his life, when he was immersed in what he later felt were the introverted concerns of monastic life. Merton the artist would have known of the artist's technique of push and pull in working on a canvas in order to achieve a final pleasing painting. He must have seen how it worked against him in the case of the monastery versus the world – the push of one and the pull of the other.

His concerns in relation to poverty, racism, warfare, the increasing pace and busyness of the world we live in, the dehumanisation of the then developing modern technologies claimed more and more of his attention in his final years.

I can only surmise that Merton would be vocal and interesting on the effects of technology in our world today and that he would be steeped in the ecological issues of the day if he were still around. One can also imagine that he would probably have been invited as a *peritus* or observer to the recent synod on the Amazon called by Pope Francis. One can lose oneself in imagining further that, as in the case of Newman, Pope Francis, an admirer of Merton, might well have honoured Merton the ageing monk by making him a cardinal.

A sign of respect for Merton's advanced social consciousness is clear with his invitation to offer a prayer for peace in 1962. He wrote:

> Save us then from our obsessions! Open our eyes, dissipate our confusions, teach us to understand ourselves and our adversary.[3]

His words are not cloaked in pleasing piety, but are simple and direct and like many a prophet's words make for uncomfortable reading.

As a young seminarian, as a priest and in recent times, one of the key attractions for me in Merton is the direct quality in his prayers. I find it in his famous vocation prayer. I quote it in full as it always seems to awaken me to reality, like a great splash of water to the face:

> My Lord God,
> I have no idea where I am going.
> I do not see the road ahead of me.
> I cannot know for certain where it will end.
> nor do I really know myself,
> and the fact that I think I am following your will
> does not mean that I am actually doing so.
> But I believe that the desire to please you
> does in fact please you.
> And I hope I have that desire in all that I am doing.
> I hope that I will never do anything apart from that
> desire.
> And I know that if I do this you will lead me by the
> right road,
> though I may know nothing about it.
> Therefore will I trust you always though
> I may seem to be lost and in the shadow of death.
> I will not fear, for you are ever with me,
> and you will never leave me to face my perils alone.
> Amen![4]

Contemplative Prayer for All

I am always drawn back to Merton's interest in and love of prayer, contemplation and the life of solitude as the atmosphere and environment in which to find such prayer. The call to the desert was a call to self-emptying that leads to 'a purity of heart' for what Merton calls 'seeing things as the Lord sees them'.[5] It was of course the monastic way of life that enabled him to pursue this in a serious way.

It has been said that 'solitude is the audience chamber of God'[6] and certain forms of prayer need that prolonged solitude in the presence of the Lord to make genuine and real progress in the spiritual life. For poor Merton it must have been like being on the rack; he was drawn to the life of solitude but at the same time was becoming the 'hermit of Times Square', in communication with more and more people because of his writing – the push and pull.[7]

The most important element for me was that he put forward and promoted the idea that contemplation was not just the preserve of priests, sisters, brothers and professed religious, but was for everyone. This led to a huge interest in courses on spirituality and spiritual direction and to this day we are reaping the benefits of that in our parishes.

In an often-cited quote, theologian Karl Rahner said, 'The devout Christian of the future will either be a "mystic", one who has experienced "something", or he will cease to be anything at all.'[8] I feel that Merton would concur with him. It was this that he was trying to achieve in his multiple books on prayer, meditation and contemplation.

Revival of Interest in Monastic Life

In recent years there has been a great interest and curiosity in relation to monasticism, with a proliferation of videos, documentaries and interviews with people living the various monastic rules. I think in particular of the film *Of Gods and Men* (2010) about a small group of Trappist monks in Algeria who lost their lives in 1996 during the civil war there. Thomas Merton helped in no small way to lead the revival and renewal of monasticism in the post-Vatican-II Church. In our own diocese of Killaloe, we are blessed by the prayerful presence of the Poor Clare Sisters in Ennis and the Cistercian Monastery in Roscrea.

A direct link between Roscrea monastery and Gethsemani was Roscrea's own Dom Eugene Boylan renowned for his own spiritual writings and as a retreat director. Eugene Boylan conducted a retreat in Gethsemani in 1958 and would have met Merton. The two had much in common as writers and spiritual thinkers of renown. They both died young (Boylan in 1964 aged sixty and Merton in 1968 aged fifty-three) and sadly we do not have any account of what Boylan made of Merton, which would be most interesting. Merton, on the other hand, is said to have thought well of Boylan as a retreat director and is reputed to have said that Boylan's retreat was the best he had made in Gethsemani.

The abbot of Mount Melleray, Richard Purcell (former abbot of Roscrea) has remarked that people are more than curious about the fact that some take the extraordinary step to live 'as hermits in community'. They are in awe of people (male and female) who are prepared to abandon the routine and nature of this world to become 'professional prayers'.[9] It remains as true today as it did in Merton's time that permanent commitment to a life of perpetual vows is seen as a witness of tremendous sacrifice to the outside observer.

Outreach

Following the runaway success of *The Seven Storey Mountain*, Merton developed an enormous capacity to correspond with people on all levels, similar to St John Henry Newman. The publication of his journals, letters and correspondence testify to that. His missionary outreach and genuine friendship with people, especially those outside the faith, of other religious traditions and those in the literary and artistic world, was immense and garnered huge respect for the Church.

In the latter years of his life, from around 1948 onwards, Merton acted as a bridge between the monastic world and the world outside the monastery through his outreach, his writing, correspondence, social and interreligious interests and retreats. A significant part of Merton's outreach to the wider world came with the development in ecumenism and interreligious dialogue after the Second Vatican Council. Merton had a developing and intense interest in the wisdom and prayer traditions of other religions. Merton sought to always learn and never to be intransigent in the face of learning that might increase his own spiritual life. He supports this view by quoting from Sufi writings:

Avoid three kinds of Master;
Those who esteem only themselves,
For their self-esteem is blindness;
Those who esteem only innovations,
For their opinions are aimless,
Without meaning;
Those who esteem only what is established;
Their minds
Are little cells of ice.[10]

Michael Ford highlights the interfaith nature of Merton's work and suggests that Merton never crossed the line of respect for his own or other faith traditions:

> But as a pioneer of interfaith dialogue he was never a syncretist and knew the limits of ecumenism. Fundamentally what he learnt from other religions improved his understanding of his own tradition. Merton represented the beginning of an era in which the quest for the integration of the contemplative and the prophetic, between mysticism and politics was viewed as an increasingly central dimension in Christian life.[11]

Role Model

Growing up as a young boy in rural Ireland at the tail end of an old form of Church – Pre-Vatican II – I used to accompany my grandfather to Benediction and Rosary on Sunday evenings. The logistical placings of the congregation reflected the clear segregation of the sexes, with women invariably on the left and men on the right. I speak of this division merely to emphasise the distinctly separate but equally strong devotional practice among both men and women at the time. My grandfather often spoke to me about the separate devotions of the Men's sodalities and the Women's sodalities. I always noted the devotion of the older men on those Sunday evenings, their respect for the sacred and the piety that was so natural to them. It was a devotion not worn on their sleeves but it was an accepted vital element of their make-up. I mention male devotion in particular simply because of my awareness then of its importance to the men in my life – my father, grandfather, uncles. I sensed that, like Patrick Kavanagh's mother, the men in my life lived an integrated form of spirituality in their lives:

> Going to second Mass on a summer Sunday –
> You meet me and you say:
> 'Don't forget to see about the cattle –'
> Among your earthiest words the angels stray.[12]

The post-Benediction talks among the men on those summer evenings quickly reverted to other important farming matters and the affairs of the world. They talked in earthiest words but what went on during the holy devotions remained in the background of their lives. Their souls were somehow the better for the exercise of religious ritual while they went back to entertaining the mundane concerns of the everyday.

The model of Church at that time has evolved into the new awareness of the role of laity since Vatican II, even though it is still a predominantly male-run church due, many would say, to some of its doctrinal bias against women. Yet, there is that ongoing anomaly of the predominance of women in the active life of the Church. Likewise, I often feel that men leave it to women when it comes to matters of Church and I feel that male spirituality has weakened as a result. It is something that I believe Thomas Merton would have engaged with had he lived and I think he would have challenged society and many world religions for their lack of inclusivity.

Merton was catholic in outlook in the sense that he embraced a wide-ranging dimension of spiritual growth and development. He lived and worked out of a male environment (monastery) and like many of us Church-men he too took for granted the gender divisions and inequalities of the Church. If there is any one area of Church life that is rich with feminine giftedness it is the area of spirituality and it is an area wherein lies the potential for spiritual growth for all the faithful.

I think perhaps that men today are slower to engage with personal spirituality and tend to see it as the domain of the cleric and women. Richard Rohr has written and spoken eloquently of the need to revive a 'male piety' and for young boys to see their fathers as religious role models for them so that they might be led to explore what their faith has to offer today and for future times. In my view Merton is an excellent role model for a revival of what I might tentatively term 'male spirituality'. As a young man I related to his story and found many of his interests and pursuits in college and beyond most interesting, his pursuit of athletics, games, publications, literature, his interest in politics and world affairs. I have no hankering for a return to the devotional environment of my grandfather's time or a desire to create a modern-day version of a *Boys' Own* spirituality, but I do think that male spirituality needs some form of revival the beginning of which might lie in an exploration of Merton's life and work.

A Call to Disappear

Jim Forest suggests that the continuing appeal of Thomas Merton lies in the fact that he is someone who is very relatable to as a man:

> We recognize in him someone whose struggles with various demons (success, fame, sensual pleasures, the quest for greener pastures) are not hugely different from our own.[13]

My own experience of discovering Merton in my late teens leaves me in full agreement with that assessment of his ongoing appeal. I am never surprised when people tell me that on re-opening a book by Merton years after first reading it they find it as fresh as before, if not fresher. They find that, like good wine, Merton has aged well. Of course, the truth lies in a fusion of Merton's work and the matured wine of their experience.

I think this is most true of *The Seven Storey Mountain* – the book of a lifetime for many people. I thought that I had perhaps outgrown the book over the years, but I have found it even more rewarding to read at this point in my life. Therefore, I conclude this voyage of rediscovery of Merton by once more paying my respects to *The Seven Storey Mountain* in the hope that you will be prompted to read it for a first time or as a return reader.

Merton's autobiography is the gateway for many to Merton's other works – works that brought great richness and above all peace into the lives of many people. It is the *pax intrantibus* that brings them into Merton's world and by spiritual osmosis into their own world. I see *The Seven Storey Mountain* as a template odyssey for the journey of my less significant life. Its wisdom re-echoes the idealism of youth, but reignites a more mature idealism that supports a life of ongoing faith. I am still enthralled by the perseverance in the faith displayed by Merton at a very conscious level from the time of his conversion, but also at a deeper unconscious level at the very core of his being since his life's journey first began.

With each revisit, I rediscover the ingrained humility of the man who selflessly abandoned a successful and promising career for a life of submission to a sometimes-fatuous authority (of the 'Father Superior knows best' variety). Merton was never blindly obedient but humbly so, in the knowledge that it brought its own peace.

Like many, I have found once more the disturbing call to solitude that is at the heart of all our spiritual lives. The call to solitude is one that we tend to see as an adolescent-like phase that we outgrow with the passage of time; however, it recurs time and time again because we know in our hearts that it is at the heart of all Christian life.

Much of the writing time of this book is taking place against the backdrop of the Covid-19 lockdown. An article by Gregory Hillis in *America* magazine suggests that because of this present crisis, 'We're all monks now.' He and a Cistercian monk, Fr Casagram, suggest that Thomas Merton saw the world as being designed:

> to distract us from thinking about questions of ultimate importance and particularly from thinking about our

mortality. Forced isolation, on the other hand, 'is making us face our own thoughts, deal with our own feelings,' said Father Casagram. 'We can run from these or we can learn from what they are telling us, both good and bad.'[14]

Rereading *The Seven Storey Mountain* has renewed my hope in the human spirit in the face of adversity and it is my prayer that our reflective monastic side will enable us to climb our single-storey mountain in these challenging times.

Thomas Merton's life and the work of his short lifetime continue to be studied at all levels of society – church and secular – he is the subject of numerous books, articles and academic theses. There would seem to be no end to this interest in the man. My sole purpose in adding to the load of work on Merton is to acknowledge my personal indebtedness for all I have harvested from his wisdom and insights during my life to date.

My own life has been enriched through living with Merton in it. He is challenging in so many ways and makes one uncomfortable in those moments when complacency creeps in. He builds you up with his store of scriptural wisdom but he will not allow you to mistake prayer or spirituality for a Tower of Babel of your own making. In other words, he is driven by a quest for authenticity and challenges us to search for sincerity and truth.

He has the zeal of the convert but is equally consumed by a lifetime's love for God and all of humanity. Above all, he has feet of clay and his frailty shines through at all times – his incompleteness completes him as a human being. I would love to have met him and enjoyed the happy gregariousness of his laughing presence that bestowed a sense of total acceptance on all who met him.

Merton's last recorded words on the day he died, 'I will disappear now,' unintentionally reflect a prophetic and deeper meaning. Despite his fame and worldly recognition, he was always alert to the saintliness of living below the radar in the obscurity of life's ordinariness – the bloom-where-planted syndrome – and believed that it behoves the true saint to regularly disappear from sight to the place where true peace smiles.

> He walked with God and was seen no more because God took him.[15]

---

[1] Robert Inchausti, *Thinking through Thomas Merton: Contemplation for Contemporary Times*, Albany: State University of New York Press, 2014, p. 35.

[2] Quoted in Sisters of Notre Dame of Chardon, Ohio, *Saints and Feast Days*, Chicago: Loyola Press, 1985, p. 38.

[3] Prayer composed by Thomas Merton that was read in the House of Representatives in Washington; *Congressional Record: Proceedings and Debates*, Vol. 108, Part 5, p. 6937, 18 April 1962, https://www.govinfo.gov/content/pkg/GPO-CRECB-1962-pt5/pdf/GPO-CRECB-1962-pt5-10-1.pdf

[4] *Thoughts in Solitude*, p. 89.

[5] 'The Recovery of Paradise', in Patrick F. O'Connell (ed.), *Thomas Merton: Selected Essays*, New York: Orbis Books, 2013, pp. 52–3.

[6] Walter Savage Landor, English writer and poet, 1775–1864; quoted in Jonathan Sacks, 'Belonging and Believing' in *Community of Faith*, London: Halban Books, 2013.

[7] Donald Graystone, *Thomas Merton and the Noonday Demon: The Camaldoli Correspondence*, Eugene, OR: Cascade Books, 2015, p. 48.

[8] Karl Rahner, 'Christian Living Formerly and Today', in David Bourke (trans.), *Theological Investigations VII*, New York: Herder and Herder, 1971, p. 15.

[9] Quotation from a talk delivered by Abbott Richard Purcell at a conference on Merton, held in Dublin in 2016, called *Thomas Merton: The Re-making of a Monk*. A recording of all talks from the conference is available as a 5-CD set from www.eist.ie.

[10] From 'To a Novice' in *Collected Poems of Thomas Merton* and also *Raids on the Unspeakable*, p. 148.

[11] Michael Ford, *Spiritual Masters for All Seasons*, New Jersey: Hidden Spring, 2009, p. 49; 'Syncretist': someone who combines different beliefs.

[12] From Patrick Kavanagh, 'In Memory of My Mother', *Collected Poems*, Antoinette Quinn (ed.), Allen Lane, 2004, p. 129.

[13] Jim Forest, *Living with Wisdom: A Life of Thomas Merton*, New York: Orbis Books, 2008, p. 245.

[14] Gregory Hillis, 'We're all monks now', *America*, 22 April 2020, https://www.americamagazine.org/faith/2020/04/22/were-all-monks-now

[15] The verse on the back of Merton's ordination card; quoted in Patrick Hart (ed.), *Thomas Merton, Monk: A Monastic Tribute*, Michigan: Cistercian Publications, 1983, p. 158.

CHAPTER EIGHT

Reading Choices

Choosing a selection from Merton's extraordinary literary legacy is difficult as, inevitably, it is a matter of personal choice. I have selected some pieces that continually appeal to me and offer them with the proviso that selected isolated excerpts, inspiring and lovely as they may be, are no substitute for reading the full parent piece.

I have also included excerpts from some of his poetry, as well as full poems. Merton himself said that he could not really master writing verse until he became a Catholic. It seems that Merton poetised only against that background of lived and reflected-on faith. Somehow his faith enabled him to bring the deeper feelings of life to the surface with the clarity that is peculiar to all good poets. It helps to bear in mind that Merton's poetry is thus charged by faith; it is, in the words of Gerard Manley Hopkins, 'charged with the grandeur of God'.[1]

I hope my selection of personal favourites will encourage you to embark on your own voyage through Merton's work. I find nothing he wrote ever less than satisfying – bon voyage!

THE BOOK OF LIFE

Either you look at the universe as a very poor creation out of which no one can make anything, or you look at your own life and your own part in the universe as infinitely rich, full of inexhaustible interest, opening out into the infinite further possibilities for study and contemplation and interest and praise. Beyond all and in all is God. Perhaps the book of life, in the end, is the book one has lived. If one has lived nothing, one is not in the book of life. I have always wanted to write about everything. That does not mean to write a book that covers everything – which would be impossible, but a book in which everything can go. A book with a little of everything that creates itself out of nothing. That has its own life. A faithful book. I can no longer look at it as a 'book'.[2]

MERCY WITHIN MERCY

What was cruel has become merciful. What is now merciful was never cruel. I have always overshadowed Jonas with my mercy, and cruelty I know not at all. Have you had sight of Me, Jonas, my child? Mercy within mercy within mercy. I have forgotten the universe without end, because I have never known sin.[3]

PRAYER FOR GOD'S MERCY

Lord have mercy.
Have mercy on my darkness, my weakness, my confusion.
Have mercy and my infidelity, my cowardice, my turning about in circles, my wandering, my evasions.
I do not ask for anything but such mercy, always, in everything, mercy.
My life here – a little solidity and very much ashes.
Almost everything is ashes. What I have prized most is ashes.
What I have attended to least is, perhaps, a little solid.
Lord have mercy. Guide me, make me want again to be holy, to be a man of God, even though in desperateness and confusion.
I do not necessarily ask for charity, a plain way, but only to go according to your love, to follow your mercy, to trust in your mercy.
I want to seek nothing at all, if this is possible. But only to be led without looking and without seeking. For thus to seek is to find.[4]

THE SEARCH FOR TRUE JOY

The only true joy on earth is to escape from the prison of our own false self and enter by love into union with the life who dwells and sings within the essence of every creature and in the core of our own souls. In His love we possess all things and enjoy fruition of them, finding Him in them all. And thus as we go about the world, everything we meet and everything we see and hear and touch, far from defiling, purifies us and plants in us something more of contemplation and of heaven.

Short of this perfection, created things do not bring us joy but pain. Until we love God perfectly, everything in the world will be able to hurt us. And the greatest misfortune is to be dead to the pain they inflict on us, and not realize what it is.[5]

HIDE AND SEEK

When I reveal most, I hide most.[6]

CONTEMPLATION

Contemplation is more than a consideration of abstract truths about God, more even than affective meditation on the things we believe. It is awakening, enlightenment and the amazing intuitive grasp by which love gains certitude of God's creative and dynamic intervention in our daily life. Hence contemplation does not simply 'find' a clear idea of God and confine Him within the limits of that idea, and hold him there as a prisoner to whom it can always return. On the contrary, contemplation is carried away by Him into His own realm, His own mystery and His own freedom. It is a pure and virginal knowledge, poor in concepts, poorer still in reasoning, but able by its very poverty and purity, to follow the Word 'wherever He may go'.[7]

ON SOLITUDE

Some men have perhaps become hermits with the thought that sanctity could only be attained by escape from other men. But the only justification for a life of deliberate solitude is the conviction that it will help you to love not only God but also other men. If you go into the desert merely to get away from people you dislike, you will find neither peace nor solitude; you will only isolate yourself with a tribe of devils.

Man seeks unity because he is the image of the One God. Unity implies solitude, and hence the need to be physically alone. But unity and solitude are not metaphysical isolation. He who isolates himself in order to enjoy a kind of independence in his egotistical and external self does not find unity at all, for he disintegrates into a multiplicity of conflicting passions and finally ends in confusion and total unreality. Solitude is not and can never be a narcissistic dialogue of the ego with itself.[8]

SOLITUDE

Solitude is as necessary for society as silence is for language and air for the lungs and food for the body.[9]

CRITIQUE OF THE BUSINESS WORLD

Businesses are, in reality, quasi-religious sects. When you go to work in one you embrace a *new faith*. And if they are really big businesses, you progress from faith to a kind of mystique. Belief in the product, preaching the product, in the end the product becomes the focus of a transcendental experience. Through the 'product' one communes with the vast forces of life, nature and history that are expressed in business. Why not face it? Advertising treats all products with the reverence and the seriousness due to sacraments.[10]

WHAT MESSAGE OF HOPE
A CONTEMPLATIVE CAN OFFER

The message of hope the contemplative offers you ... is not that you need to find your way through the jungle of language and problems that today surround God: but whether you understand or not, God loves you, is present to you, lives in you, dwells in you, calls you, saves you, and offers you an understanding and light which are like nothing you ever found in books or heard in sermons. The contemplative has nothing to tell you except to reassure you and say that, if you dare to penetrate your own silence and risk the sharing of that solitude with the lonely other who seeks God through you, then you will truly recover the light and the capacity to understand what is beyond words and beyond explanations because it is too close to be explained: it is the intimate union in the depth of your own heart of God's spirit and your own secret inmost self, so that you and He are in all truth One Spirit.[11]

COSMIC DANCE

When we are alone on a starlit night, when by chance we see the migrating birds in autumn descending on a grove of junipers to rest and eat; when we see children in a moment when they are really children, when we know love in our hearts; or when, like the Japanese poet Bashō we hear an old frog land in a quiet pond with a solitary splash – at such times the awakening, the tuning inside out of all values, the 'newness', the emptiness and the purity of vision that make themselves evident, all these provided glimpse of the cosmic dance.[12]

PRIESTHOOD

My priestly ordination was, I felt, the one great secret for which I had been born. Ten years before I was ordained, when I was in the world, and seemed to be one of the men in the world most unlikely to become a priest, I had suddenly realized that for me ordination to the priesthood was, in fact, a matter of life or death, heaven or hell. As I finally came within sight of this perfect meeting with the inscrutable will of God, my vocation became clear. It was a mercy and a secret which were so purely mine that at first I intended to speak of them to no one.

Yet because no man is ordained priest for himself alone, since my priesthood made me belong not only to God but also to all men, it was fitting that I should have spoken a little of what was in my heart to my friends who came to my ordination.[13]

CLEARING THE CLUTTER OF THE MODERN WORLD

The greatest need of our time is to clean out the enormous mass of mental and emotional rubbish that clutters our minds and makes all political and social life a mass illness. Without the house cleaning we cannot begin to see. Unless we see, we cannot think. The purification must begin with the mass media. How?[14]

TECHNOLOGICAL IMPERATIVE

It does us no good to make fantastic progress if we do not know how to live with it, if we cannot make good use of it, and if, in fact, our technology becomes nothing more than an expensive and complicated way of cultural disintegration. It is bad form to say such things, to recognize such possibilities. But they are possibilities, and they are not often intelligently taken into account. People get emotional about them from time to time, and then try to sweep them aside into forgetfulness. The fact remains that we have created for ourselves a culture which is not yet livable for mankind as a whole.[15]

EVENTS AND PSEUDO EVENTS

I have watched TV twice in my life. I am frankly not terribly interested in TV anyway. Certainly I do not pretend that by simply refusing to keep up with the latest news I am therefore unaffected by what goes on, or free of it all. Certain events happen and they affect me as they do other people. It is important for me to know about them too. But I refrain from trying to know them in their fresh condition as 'news'. When they reach me they have become slightly stale. I eat the same tragedies as others but in the form of tasteless crusts. The news reaches me in the long run through books and magazines, and no longer as a stimulant. Living without news is like living without cigarettes (another peculiarity of the monastic life). The need for this habitual indulgence quickly disappears. So when you hear news without the 'need' to hear it, it treats you differently. And you treat it differently too.[16]

AMERICA IN 1967

I love the people I run into, but I pity them for having to live as they do, and I think the world of USA in 1967 is a world of crass, blind, overstimulated, phony, lying, stupidity. The war in Asia slowly gets worse – and almost more inane. The temper of the country is one of blindness, fat, self-satisfied, ruthless, mindless corruption. A lot of people are uneasy about it but helpless to do anything against it. The rest are perfectly content with the rat race, as it is, and with its competitive, acquisitive, hurtling, souped-up drive into nowhere. A massively aimless, baseless, shrewd cockiness that simply exalts itself without purpose. The mindless orgasm, in which there is no satisfaction, only spasm.[17]

SANITY

The generals and fighters on both sides, in World War II, the ones who carried out the total destruction of entire cities, these were the sane ones. Those who have invented and developed atomic bombs, thermonuclear bombs, missiles; who have planned the strategy of the next war; who have evaluated the various possibilities of using bacterial and chemical agents: these are not the crazy people, they are the sane people. The ones who coolly estimate how many millions of victims can be considered expendable in a nuclear war, I presume they do all right with the Rorschach ink blots too. On the other hand, you will probably find that the pacifists and the ban-the-bomb people are, quite seriously ... a little crazy. I am beginning to realize that 'sanity' is no longer a value or an end in itself. The 'sanity' of modern man is about as useful to him as the huge bulk and muscles of the dinosaur. If he were a little less sane, a little more doubtful, a little more aware of his absurdities and contradictions, perhaps there might be a possibility of his survival. But if he is sane, too sane ... perhaps we must say that in a society like ours the worst insanity is to be totally without anxiety, totally 'sane'.[18]

POETRY

St Malachy

In November, in the days to remember the dead
When air smells cold as earth,
St Malachy, who is very old, gets up,
Parts the thin curtains of trees and dawns upon our land.

His coat is filled with drops of rain, and he is bearded
With all the seas of Poseidon.
(Is it a crozier, or a trident in his hand?)
He weeps against the gothic windows, and the empty cloister
Mourns like an ocean shell.

Two bells in the steeple
Talk faintly to the old stranger
And the tower considers his waters.
'I have been sent to see my festival,' (his cavern speaks!)

'For I am the saint of the day.
Shall I shake the drops from my locks and stand in your transept,
Or, leaving you, rest in the silence of my history?'

So the bells rang and we opened the antiphoners
And the wrens and larks flew up out of the pages.
Our thoughts became lambs. Our hearts swam like seas.
One monk believed that we should sing to him
Some stone-age hymn
Or something in the giant language.
So we played to him in the plainsong of the giant Gregory
And oceans of Scripture sang upon bony Eire.

Then the last salvage of flowers
(Fostered under glass after the gardens foundered)
Held up their little lamps on Malachy's altar
To peer into his wooden eyes before the Mass began.

Rain sighed down the sides of the stone church.
Storms sailed by all day in battle fleets.
At five o'clock, when we tried to see the sun, the speechless visitor
Sighed and arose and shook the humus from his feet
And with his trident stirred our trees
And left down-wood, shaking some drops upon the ground.

Thus copper flames fall, tongues of fire fall
The leaves in hundreds fall upon his passing
While night sends down her dreadnought darkness
Upon this spurious Pentecost.

And the Melchisedec of our year's end
Who came without a parent, leaves without a trace,
And rain comes rattling down upon our forest
Like the doors of a country jail.

A Psalm

When psalms surprise me with their music
And antiphons turn to rum
The Spirit sings: the bottom drops out of my soul.

And from the center of my cellar, Love, louder than thunder
Opens a heaven of naked air.

New eyes awaken.
I send Love's name into the world with wings
And songs grow up around me like a jungle.
Choirs of all creatures sing the tunes
Your Spirit played in Eden.
Zebras and antelopes and birds of paradise
Shine on the face of the abyss
And I am drunk with the great wilderness
Of the sixth day in Genesis.

But sound is never half so fair
As when that music turns to air
And the universe dies of excellence.

Sun, moon and stars
Fall from their heavenly towers.
Joys walk no longer down the blue world's shore.

Though fires loiter, lights still fly on the air of the gulf,
All fear another wind, another thunder:
Then one more voice
Snuffs all their flares in one gust.

And I go forth with no more wine and no more stars
And no more buds and no more Eden
And no more animals and no more sea:

While God sings by himself in acres of night
And walls fall down, that guarded Paradise.

The Flight into Egypt
Through every precinct of the wintry city
Squadroned iron resounds upon the streets;
Herod's police
Make shudder the dark steps of the tenements
At the business about to be done.

Neither look back upon Thy starry country,
Nor hear what rumors crowd across the dark
Where blood runs down those holy walls,
Nor frame a childish blessing with Thy hand
Towards that fiery spiral of exulting souls!

Go, Child of God, upon the singing desert,
Where, with eyes of flame,
The roaming lion keeps thy road from harm.

Song for Our Lady of Cobre
The white girls stir their heads like trees,
The black girls go
Reflected like flamingoes in the street.

The white girls sing as shrill as water,
The black girls talk as quiet as clay.

The white girls open their arms like clouds,
The black girls close their eyes like wings;
Angels bow down like bells,
Angels look up like toys,

Because the heavenly stars
Stand in a ring:
And all the pieces of the mosaic, earth,
Get up and fly away like birds.

For My Brother: Reported Missing in Action, 1943

Sweet brother, if I do not sleep
My eyes are flowers for your tomb;
And if I cannot eat my bread,
My fasts shall live like willows where you died.
If in the heat I find no water for my thirst,
My thirst shall turn to springs for you, poor traveller.

Where, in what desolate and smokey country,
Lies your poor body, lost and dead?
And in what landscape of disaster
Has your unhappy spirit lost its road?

Come, in my labor find a resting place
And in my sorrows lay your head,
Or rather take my life and blood
And buy yourself a better bed

- Or take my breath and take my death
And buy yourself a better rest.

When all the men of war are shot
And flags have fallen into dust,
Your cross and mine shall tell men still
Christ died on each, for both of us.

For in the wreckage of your April Christ lies slain,
And Christ weeps in the ruins of my spring:
The money of Whose tears shall fall
Into your weak and friendless hand,
And buy you back to your own land:

The silence of Whose tears shall fall
Like bells upon your alien tomb.
Hear them and come: they call you home.

PRAYERS

Prayer for Peace
A day of ominous decision has now dawned on this free nation.
Save us then from our obsessions! Open our eyes, dissipate our confusions,
teach us to understand ourselves and our adversary.
Let us never forget that sins against the law of love
are punishable by loss of faith, and those without faith
stop at no crime to achieve their ends!
Help us to be masters of the weapons that threaten to master us.
Help us to use our science for peace and plenty, not for war and destruction.
Save us from the compulsion to follow our adversaries in all that we most hate,
confirming them in their hatred and suspicion of us.
Resolve our inner contradictions,
which now grow beyond belief and beyond bearing.
They are at once a torment and a blessing:
for if you had not left us the light of conscience,
we would not have to endure them.
Teach us to wait and trust.
Grant light, grant strength and patience to all who work for peace.
But grant us above all to see that our ways are not necessarily your ways,
that we cannot fully penetrate the mystery of your designs
and that the very storm of power now raging on this earth
reveals your hidden will and your inscrutable decision.
Grant us to see your face in the lightning of this cosmic storm.[19]

Prayer to the Good Shepherd
Good Shepherd, you have a wild and crazy sheep in love with thorns and brambles. But please don't get tired of looking for me! I know You won't. For You have found me. All I have to do is stay found.[20]

The Merton Prayer

> My Lord God,
> I have no idea where I am going.
> I do not see the road ahead of me.
> I cannot know for certain where it will end.
> nor do I really know myself,
> and the fact that I think I am following your will
> does not mean that I am actually doing so.
> But I believe that the desire to please you
> does in fact please you.
> And I hope I have that desire in all that I am doing.
> I hope that I will never do anything apart from that
> desire.
> And I know that if I do this you will lead me by the
> right road,
> though I may know nothing about it.
> Therefore will I trust you always though
> I may seem to be lost and in the shadow of death.
> I will not fear, for you are ever with me,
> and you will never leave me to face my perils alone.[21]

[1] Gerard Manley Hopkins, 'God's Grandeur', *The Works of Gerard Manley Hopkins*, London: Wordsworth Editions, 1994, p. 26.

[2] Journal entry, 17 July 1956, in Patrick Hart and Jonathan Montaldo (eds), *The Intimate Merton: His Life from His Journals*, Oxford: Lion Publishing, 2000.

[3] Journal entry, 4 July 1952, *Entering the Silence: Volume II, 1941–1952*, p. 488.

[4] Journal entry, 2 August 1960, journal entry, in *Turning Toward the World: The Pivotal Years (Journals, IV: 1960–1963)*, 1996, p. 28.

[5] *New Seeds of Contemplation*, p. 25.

[6] Thomas Merton quoted in the preface of Michael Mott, *The Seven Mountains of Thomas Merton*, Boston: Houghton Mifflin, 1984.

[7] *New Seeds of Contemplation*, p. 5.

[8] *New Seeds of Contemplation*, p. 52.

[9] *No Man is an Island*, p. 260.

[10] *Conjecture of a Guilty Bystander*, p. 232.

[11] *The Hidden Ground of Love: Letters on Religious Experience and Social Concerns (Letters I)*, 1985, pp. 170–1.

[12] *New Seeds of Contemplation*, p. 296–7.

[13] *The Sign of Jonas*, p. 177.

[14] *Conjectures of a Guilty Bystander*; quoted in Robert Inchausti (ed.), *The Pocket Thomas Merton*, Boston: New Seeds, 2005, p. 47.

[15] Ibid., p. 51.

[16] *Faith and Violence*; quoted in Inchausti, *The Pocket Thomas Merton*, p. 60.

[17] Journal of Thomas Merton, 27 May 1967, Volume 6, Learning to Love

[18] *A Devout Meditation in Memory of Adolf Eichmann*, Kentucky: Abbey of Gethsemani, 1966; quoted in *Raids on the Unspeakable*.

[19] Adapted from prayer composed by Thomas Merton that was read in the House of Representatives in Washington; *Congressional Record: Proceedings and Debates*, Vol. 108, Part 5, p. 6937, 18 April 1962, https://www.govinfo.gov/content/pkg/GPO-CRECB-1962-pt5/pdf/GPO-CRECB-1962-pt5-10-1.pdf

[20] Journal entry, Good Shepherd Sunday 1948; quoted in John Moses, *Divine Discontent: The Prophetic Voice of Thomas Merton*, London: Bloomsbury, 2014, p. 29.

[21] Thomas Merton, *Thoughts in Solitude*, New York: Farrar, Strauss and Giroux, 1999, p. 79.

Bibliography

WORKS OF THOMAS MERTON

Autobiographies
The Seven Storey Mountain, New York: Harcourt Brace, 1948.
Elected Silence, Dublin: Clonmore and Reynolds, 1949.
The Sign of Jonas, London: Hollis and Carter, 1953.
A Secular Journal, London: Catholic Book Club, 1959.
The Waters of Siloe, New York: Harcourt Brace, 1949.

Biblical Topics
Bread in the Wilderness, Kent: Burns and Oates, 1953.
The Living Bread, Dublin: Clonmore and Reynolds, 1956.
Praying the Psalms, Minnesota: Liturgical Press, 1956.
He is Risen. Dublin: Argus Communications, 1975.

Biographies
Exile Ends in Glory: The Life of a Trappistine, Mother M. Berchmans, O.C.S.O., Wisconson: Bruce Publishing Company, 1948.
What Are These Wounds?: The Life of a Cistercian Mystic, Saint Lutgarde of Aywières, Dublin: Clonmore and Reynolds, 1948.
The Last of the Fathers: Saint Bernard of Clairvaux and the Encyclical Letter, Doctor Mellifluus, London: Harcourt Brace, 1954.

Contemplation and Meditation
Seeds of Contemplation, England: Burns and Oates, 1961.
The Ascent to Truth, England: Burns and Oates, 1951.
Disputed Questions, New York: Farrar, Straus and Cudahy, 1960.

New Seeds of Contemplation, London: Burns and Oates, 1962.

Raids on the Unspeakable, London: Burns and Oates, 1966.

Conjectures of a Guilty Bystander, New York: Doubleday, 1965.

The Climate of Monastic Prayer, Minnesota: Liturgical Press, 2018 (first published 1968); Republished in the UK as *Where Prayer Flourishes*, London: Canterbury Press, 2018.

Contemplative Prayer, New York: Herder and Herder, 1969.

What is Contemplation, Illinois: Templegate, 1978 (first published 1950).

Eastern Thought

The Way of Chuang Tzu, New York: New Directions, 1965.

Mystics and Zen Masters, New York: Delta, 1967.

Zen and the Birds of Appetite, Boston: Shambhala, 1993.

Thoughts on the East, New York: Burns and Oates, 1995.

Journal Writings

The Secular Journal of Thomas Merton, New York: Farrar, Straus and Cudahy, 1959.

The Asian Journal of Thomas Merton, New York: New Directions, 1973.

Edited Journals

Run to the Mountain: The Story of a Vocation (The Journal of Thomas Merton, Volume 1: 1939–1941), Patrick Hart (ed.), San Francisco: HarperCollins, 1995.

Entering the Silence: Becoming a Monk and a Writer (The Journals of Thomas Merton Volume II: 1941–1952), Jonathan Montaldo (ed.), San Francisco: HarperCollins, 1997.

A Search for Solitude: Pursuing the Monk's True Life (The Journals of Thomas Merton, Volume III: 1952–1960), Laurence S. Cunningham (ed.), San Francisco: HarperCollins, 1997.

Turning Toward the World: The Pivotal Years (The Journals of Thomas Merton, Volume IV: 1960–1963), Victor A. Kramer (ed.), San Francisco: HarperCollins, 1997.

Dancing in the Water of Life, Seeking Peace in the Hermitage (The Journals of Thomas Merton Volume V: 1963–1965), Robert E. Daggy (ed.), San Francisco: HarperCollins, 1998.

Learning to Love: Exploring Solitude and Freedom (The Journals of Thomas Merton Volume VI: 1965–1967), Christine M. Bochen (ed.), San Francisco: HarperCollins, 1998.

The Other Side of the Mountain: The End of the Journey (The Journals of Thomas Merton Volume VII: 1967–1968), Patrick Hart (ed.), San Francisco: HarperCollins, 1999.

Letters
Thomas Merton: A Life In Letters, William H. Shannon and Christine M. Bochen (eds), San Francisco: HarperOne, 2008.

Monastic, Church and Spiritual Life
The Waters of Siloe, New York: Harcourt Brace, 1949.

No Man is an Island, London: Burns and Oates, 1955.

Silence in Heaven: A Book of Monastic Life, New York: Studio Publications, 1956.

The Silent Life, New York: Farrar, Straus and Cudahy, 1957.

Thoughts in Solitude, Kent: Burns and Oates, 1958.

The Wisdom of the Desert: Sayings From the Desert Fathers of the Fourth Century, London: Burns and Oates, 1997.

Spiritual Direction and Meditation, Hertfordshire: Anthony Clarke Books, 1975.

The New Man, Kent: Burns and Oates, 1962.

Life and Holiness, New York: Image Books, 1964.

Seasons of Celebration, New York: Farrar, Straus and Giroux, 1965.

Gethsemani: A Life of Praise, Kentucky: Abbey of Gethsemani, 1966.

Contemplation in a World of Action, New York: Image Books, 1973.

Cistercian Life, Cistercian Book Services, 1974.

The Monastic Journey, Patrick Hart (ed.), New York: Image Books, 1978.

Love and Living, Naomi Burton Stone and Patrick Hart, Dan Diego: Harcourt Brace Jovanovich, 1979.

Novel
My Argument with the Gestapo: A Macaronic Journal, New York: Doubleday, 1969.

Poetry

The Collected Poems of Thomas Merton, New York: New Directions, 1977.

Selected Poems of Thomas Merton, New York: New Directions, 1967.

Social Issues

Seeds of Destruction, New York: Farrar, Straus and Giroux, 1964.

Gandhi on Non-Violence, New York: New Directions, 1965.

Faith and Violence: Christian Teaching and Christian Practice, Notre Dame: University of Notre Dame Press, 1968.

The Non-Violent Alternative, New York: Farrar, Straus and Giroux, 1980 (Revised ed. of *Thomas Merton On Peace*, New York: McCall Publishing Company, 1971).

Raids on the Unspeakable, London: Burns and Oates, 1977.

Thomas Merton in Alaska: The Alaskan Conferences, Journals, and Letters, New York: New Directions, 1988.

The Hidden Ground of Love: Letters on Religious Experience and Social Concerns (Letters I), William H. Shannon (ed.), New York: Farrar, Straus and Giroux, 1985.

The Road to Joy: Letters to New and Old Friends (Letters II), Robert Daggy (ed.), New York: Farrar, Straus and Giroux, 1989.

The School of Charity: Letters on Religious Renewal and Spiritual Direction (Letters III), Patrick Hart (ed.), New York: Farrar, Straus and Giroux, 1990.

The Courage for Truth: Letters to Writers (Letters IV), Christine M. Bochen (ed.), New York: Farrar, Straus and Giroux, 1993.

Witness to Freedom: Letters in Times of Crisis (Letters V), William H. Shannon (ed.), New York: Farrar, Straus and Giroux, 1994.

The Intimate Merton: His Life from His Journals, Patrick Hart and Jonathan Montaldo (eds), Oxford: Lion Publishing, 2000.

GENERAL BIBLIOGRAPHY

Bailey, Raymond, *Thomas Merton on Mysticism*, New York: Image Books, 1974.

Bamberger, J.E., OCSO, *Thomas Merton: Prophet of Renewal*, Minnesota: Liturgical Press, 2005.

Bochen, C.M., W.H. Shannon and P.F. O'Connell (eds), *The Thomas Merton Encyclopedia*, New York: Orbis Books, 2002.

Cunningham, L.S., *Thomas Merton and the Monastic Vision*, Cambridge: William B. Eerdmans Publishing Company, 1999.

_____ (ed.), *Thomas Merton: Spiritual Master*, New York: Paulist Press, 1992.

Finley, J., *Merton's Palace of Nowhere: A Search for God through Awareness of the True Self*, Indiana: Ave Maria Press, 1978.

Ford, M., *Spiritual Masters for All Seasons*, New Jersey: Hidden Spring, 2009.

Forest, J., *Living with Wisdom: A Life of Thomas Merton*, New York: Orbis Books, 2008.

_____, *Thomas Merton: A Pictorial Biography*, New York: Paulist Press, 1980.

Fox, M., *Meister Eckhart: A Mystic-Warrior for Our Times*, California: New World Library, 2014.

Furlong, M., *Merton: A Biography*, San Francisco: Harper and Row, 1980.

Gordon, M., *On Thomas Merton*, Boulder: Shambhala, 2018.

Graystone, D., *Thomas Merton and the Noonday Demon: The Camaldoli Correspondence*, Eugene, OR: Cascade Books, 2015.

Hart, P. and J. Montaldo (eds), *The Intimate Merton: His Life from His Journals*, Oxford: Lion Publishing, 2000.

Hart, P. (ed.), *The Literary Essays of Thomas Merton*, New York: New Directions, 1981.

_____ (ed.), *Thomas Merton, Monk: A Monastic Tribute*, Michigan: Cistercian Publications, 1983.

Higgins, M.W., *Thomas Merton: Faithful Visionary*, Minnesota: Liturgical Press, 2014.

_____, *Heretic Blood: The Spiritual Geography of Thomas Merton*, Canada: Stoddart, 1998.

_____, *The Unquiet Monk: Thomas Merton's Questing Faith*, New York: Orbis Books, 2015.

Horan, D.P., OFM, *The Franciscan Heart of Thomas Merton*, Indiana: Ave Maria Press, 2014.

Inchausti, R., *Thinking through Thomas Merton: Contemplation for Contemporary Times*, Albany: State University of New York Press, 2014.

_____, *Thomas Merton's American Prophesy*, Albany: State University of New York Press, 1998.

_____ (ed.), *Echoing Silence: Thomas Merton on the Vocation of Writing*, Boston: New Seeds, 2007.

_____ (ed.), *The Pocket Thomas Merton*, Boston: New Seeds, 2005.

Lipsey, R., *Angelic Mistakes: The Art of Thomas Merton*, Boston and London: New Seeds, 2006.

Martin, J., SJ, *Becoming Who You Are: Insights from the True Self from Thomas Merton and other Saints*, Boston: Hidden Spring, 2005.

McDonnell, T.P. (ed.), *A Thomas Merton Reader*, New York: Image Books, 1974.

Montaldo, J. (ed.), *A Year with Thomas Merton: Daily Meditations from His Journals*, London: SPCK, 2005.

Moses, J., *Divine Discontent: The Prophetic Voice of Thomas Merton*, London: Bloomsbury, 2014.

Mott, M., *The Seven Mountains of Thomas Merton*, Boston: Houghton Mifflin, 1984.

O'Connell, P.F. (ed.), *Thomas Merton: Selected Essays*, New York: Orbis Books, 2013.

Pennington, M.B., OCSO, *Thomas Merton, Brother Monk: The Quest for True Freedom*, San Francisco: Harper and Row, 1987.

Rice, E., *The Man in the Sycamore Tree: The Good Times and Hard Life of Thomas Merton*, New York: Image Books, 1972.

Simsic, W., *Praying with Thomas Merton: Companions for the Journey*, Minnesota: St Mary's Press, 1994.

Shannon, W.H. and C.M. Bochen (eds), *Thomas Merton: A Life in Letters*, Oxford: Lion Publishing, 2008.

A Poem for Merton

Thomas,

The world claimed you as its own.
You allowed none but the angels to claim you.

You lie serenely entombed in your monk's habit:
At home.
Affirming what you always knew.

Sleep now Tom of the Anawim – hush-a-bye little one.
A lullaby of Kentucky guides you home